Praise for *Winning Mind*

"Simon Lancaster is a polymath – excellent civil servant, brilliant speech writer, talented musician, and fantastic author. If you want to understand why this description breeches the rhetorical device of tricolon, read this wonderful book."

–Rt. Hon Alan Johnson MP, former Home Secretary

"From substance to style, *Winning Minds* is an excellent insight into the language of leadership written in the clear yet humorous way that is Simon's hallmark."

–Richard Solomons, CEO, Intercontinental Hotels Group plc

"Simon's book unlocks the secret of how to be a world-class communicator and leader in a book that is as entertaining as it is packed with know-how."
–Darren Childs, Chief Executive Officer, UKTV

"If you need people to care as much as you care, to be moved as much as you are moved and to give as much as you give, read this simple, clear, and effective book."

-Adrienne Kelbie, Chief Executive, Disclosure and Barring Service

"*Winning Minds* lays bare with shocking clarity the simple techniques that great communicators use to manipulate our emotions. Give them a go and unleash your hidden leader!"

**–Peter Wanless, CEO, National Society for the
Prevention of Cruelty to Children**

"This brilliant business book is filled with powerful stuff that will change the way you 'think' about language and the way you 'do' leadership. Simon's superb style is somewhere between serious boardroom discussion and a cosy fireside chat. Massively entertaining. Hugely useful. Thoroughly recommended."

–Mark Swain, Director, Henley Business School

"In this friendly, accessible, and highly entertaining account of leaders' language, Simon Lancaster demonstrates many of the features of persuasive speaking in the actual style of his writing: clear, concise, and humorous.

Winning Minds wins us over by finding an adroit balance between erudition and story-telling, so that fascinating insights from neuroscience are blended with amusing anecdotes from his own experience in the world of speechwriting."

–Jonathan Charteris-Black, Professor of Linguistics,
University of the West of England

"*Winning Minds* is an important resource for all engaged in corporate communication and for anyone else who wants to be able to tell the difference between leaders and misleaders."

–Prof J. Powell and Prof. L Rubinstein, Centre for Oratory and
Rhetoric, Royal Holloway, University of London

"Simon is a gifted facilitator of executive workshops who has successfully brought his techniques to life in this engaging, challenging and inspiring book."

–Professor Clive Holtham, Cass Business School

Winning Minds

Secrets From the Language of Leadership

Simon Lancaster

palgrave
macmillan

First published 2015 by
PALGRAVE MACMILLAN

Palgrave Macmillan in the UK is an imprint of Macmillan Publishers Limited, registered in England, company number 785998, of Houndmills, Basingstoke, Hampshire RG21 6XS.

Palgrave Macmillan in the US is a division of St Martin's Press LLC, 175 Fifth Avenue, New York, NY 10010.

Palgrave Macmillan is the global academic imprint of the above companies and has companies and representatives throughout the world.

Palgrave® and Macmillan® are registered trademarks in the United States, the United Kingdom, Europe and other countries.

ISBN 978-1-137-46592-4   ISBN 978-1-137-46594-8 (eBook)
DOI 10.1057/9781137465948

This book is printed on paper suitable for recycling and made from fully managed and sustained forest sources. Logging, pulping and manufacturing processes are expected to conform to the environmental regulations of the country of origin.

A catalogue record for this book is available from the British Library.

Library of Congress Cataloging-in-Publication Data
Lancaster, Simon, 1972–
Winning minds : secrets from the language of leadership / Simon Lancaster.
pages cm

1. Communication in management.   2. Communication in organizations.
3. Leadership.   I. Title.
HD30.3.L357 2015
658.4'092—dc23   2015003457

Typeset by MPS Limited, Chennai, India.

To Lottie and Alice
Be who you want to be,
Do what you want to do,
Go where you want to go,
I'm always beside you.

Contents

List of Illustrations, Word Clouds

(All illustrations by Paul Rainey – www.pbrainey.com)

Illustrations

Word Clouds

List of Tables

Introduction

On 26 July 2012, my wife Lucy and I were in Hyde Park along with 250,000 others to celebrate the start of the London 2012 Olympic Games. It was a perfect summer day: drinks flowed, Dizzee Rascal boomed out blistering versions of 'Bassline Junkie' and 'Bonkers'... but then Boris Johnson, London's mayor, staggered on stage. The crowd murmured disapprovingly at the sight of the politician. Someone shouted 'wanker'. A few people took out their phones and pressed record.

Now, I am not a natural Boris fan. Most of my political experience was gained on the other side of the fence working with the other Johnson (Alan). However, Boris blew my socks off that day. In just three minutes, he turned the crowd from hostility to hysteria. It was a masterclass in the Language of Leadership:

> I've never seen anything like this in all my life.
>
> The excitement is growing so much I think the Geiger counter of Olympomania is going to go zoink off the scale.
>
> People are coming from around the world and they're seeing us and they're seeing the greatest city on earth, aren't they?
>
> There are some people coming from around the world who don't yet know all the preparations we've done to get London ready in the last seven years.

I hear there's a guy called Mitt Romney who wants to know whether we're ready.

Are we ready? Yes, we are.

The venues are ready. The stadium is ready. The aquatics centre is ready. The velodrome is ready. The security is ready. The police are ready. The transport system is ready. And our Team GB athletes are ready... Aren't they?

There's going to be more gold, silver, bronze medals than you'd need to bail out Greece and Spain together.

Final question. Can we put on the greatest Olympic Games that has ever been held?

Are we worried about the weather? We're not worried about the weather.

Can we beat France? Yes we can! Can we beat Australia? Yes we can! Can we beat Germany? I think we can.

Thank you very much everybody. Have a wonderful, wonderful London 2012. Thank you for all your support.

Watch it on YouTube – seriously. Watch for yourself the authentic shifts in mood. Watch the first tentative laughs. Watch how energy ripples through the crowd. Watch how everyone joins in with the 'Yes we can' refrain. Watch also how, at the end, the crowd spontaneously erupts in applause and starts chanting 'Boris! Boris! Boris!'.

Lucy and I were also chanting 'Boris! Boris!' Then we stopped. Suddenly, we returned to our senses. 'Blimey. What happened there?' said Lucy. 'Drugs', I replied. And that was it. The speech felt emotional but the reaction was chemical. A few lines of Boris had left everyone high: intoxicated and irrational. So what happened? We know what the brain looks like on heroin. Let's look at the brain on Boris.

Boris's speech stimulated the release of three powerful drugs in the brain. The first was serotonin, the self-esteem drug. Serotonin makes us feel confident, strong and powerful. Prozac and other anti-depressants mimic its effect.[1] Praise causes serotonin to be released and Boris laid it on thick with the talk about our great city, our great country and our great athletes.

The second drug he got going was oxytocin, the love drug. Oxytocin makes us feel warm, fuzzy and safe. Ecstasy mimics its effect. Oxytocin is released naturally when we feel a closeness with others – whether that comes from touching, holding hands, cuddling, having sex or, yes, even listening to a Boris speech. Boris united the crowd through his constant use of the first-person plural: his speech was all 'we', not 'me'. And it was not 'We, the Conservative Party' as you would expect from some politicians, it was 'We, Great Britain'. He also united us by reminding us who we were up against: the condescending Mitt Romney, the bankrupt states of Southern Europe and, of course – the Germans. What better way to unite 250,000 Brits than mentioning the Germans?

The third drug he stimulated was dopamine, the reward drug. Dopamine makes us feel *great*. Dopamine is the same drug that is released by taking cocaine, heroin and speed. Dopamine is released in greater or lesser quantities according to whether or not our expectations are met. Boris surpassed expectations. Instead of a self-congratulatory political speech we got a short burst of patriotic fervour, peppered with such craziness as 'Olympomania' and 'zoink'.

So, Boris's speech was just a bit like taking ecstasy, Prozac, cocaine, heroin and speed all at once. There were more drugs circulating in Hyde Park that day than when the Stones played in 1969. And the effect was amazing, leaving everyone feeling united, proud and invincible. Complete strangers greeted one another as friends, goofily exclaiming 'Good old Boris!' and 'Total legend!' The wave of euphoria was similar to a rock concert or evangelical sermon.

But then, as always, after the high comes the low. The comedown. And this is the miserable bit. Now, there are no fun drugs being released, just toxins, and they leave us feeling grim. But it is within the depths of depression that the leader draws strength. Because, as the low kicks in, so does the craving for the next high. And when we look for the high, to whom do we turn? Whoever made us high last time.

That's what draws people to their leader. They're craving pride. They're craving connection. They're craving purpose. They're addicted, junkies, hunting for their next fix. That is the secret contract upon which great leaders trade. That is what gives leaders power. I'll meet your emotional needs, but in return you give me your support. That's the contract. That's the deal. That is the basis of the Language of Leadership.

chapter 1

Winning Minds – The Secret Science of the Language of Leadership

It's Christmas 2014 and I'm in the Red Lion, a snug, warm pub in the heart of the Brecon Beacons. There's a roaring fire, I'm sitting in a big leather armchair but, although I've come here to work on the final draft of a speech about leadership, I'm not making much progress. A group of men on the table next to me are raucously arguing about how much money they would need to win on the lottery to stop work. A guy turns to me. 'What's the annual interest on a million pounds?' '£30,000?' I guess. The guy smiles. 'There. You can buy a house in Merthyr Tydfil for £30,000.' Someone snips in. 'Yes, but what would you do with the other £29,000!' More laughter. I'm invited to join their table.

Our conversation over the next two hours is like a whirlwind tour through recent history – from the mines closing in South Wales to immigration from Central and Eastern Europe to tensions with Islam. What is striking for me is how much of the conversation comes back to leaders: from Arthur Scargill ('What was going on with that scrag of hair?') to Margaret Thatcher ('She had the devil in her eyes') to Michael Heseltine ('Wasn't he into swinging?') to Barack Obama ('They said he could walk on water') to David Cameron ('I'd like to put a bullet between his eyes') to Nigel Farage ('He's a neo-Nazi. Does that matter?') to Ed Miliband ('Complete clown') and Ed Balls ('He looks like someone has shoved a pineapple up his backside').

Leaders arouse huge strength of feeling – for better or for worse. They
touch us deeply and emotionally. And, right now, there is a global
crisis in leadership.[1] It's evident in conversations like this in pubs
in Britain but also in the riots in South America and the
uprisings in the Middle East. The world needs leaders.
Without leaders, the advance of civilisation can falter.

There is a global crisis in leadership

Great leadership is intrinsically about great communication.
Branson. Obama. Jobs. Roddick. Thatcher. Blair. You can't be a great leader
without being a great communicator. But communication now is getting
harder than ever. People spend more time looking down at their phones
than up to their leaders. This is the challenge which must be overcome.

The good news is that there is a secret Language of Leadership: a secret
set of physical, verbal and vocal cues and signals that has existed for tens
of thousands of years which still determines who makes it to the top in
business and politics today. Many in the past have tried to decode this
secret language but it is only now, with recent breakthroughs in neuroscience and behavioural economics, that we can say with much greater
certainty what works and why.

This book is a user's guide to that Language of Leadership. It opens up a
treasure chest of tips, tricks and techniques which you can instantly use to
become more effective, engaging and inspiring.

But before we get to all that, let me scoop you up out of that little pub in
Wales and zip you back in time 2500 years ago to Athens: from the Red Lion
to an ancient Greek tavern. Around us now are men in togas, slurping from
urns of red wine and enjoying just the kind of indecorous conversation we
just witnessed in Wales. So let's sit down, enjoy a goblet of wine and nib-
ble on some olives. Take a look in the corner. See that earnest-looking man
scribbling away? That is Aristotle. The book he's writing is called *Rhetoric*.

Rhetoric

Despite the passage of thousands of years and the advent of all sorts of
new technologies and changes, Aristotle's *Rhetoric* is still, for me, the

ultimate guide to the art of communication. Lots of people bang on about Machiavelli and Dale Carnegie but, as far as I'm concerned, Aristotle is the master. *Rhetoric* was a work not of scientific deduction, but of observation. And what is most extraordinary is that, way back when human civilisation was just a dot, he nailed it.

Aristotle said that great communication requires three things: ethos, pathos and logos (as you'll soon discover, all great things come in threes...). Now, if those terms are all Greek to you: ethos means credibility, pathos means emotion and logos means logic, or the *appearance* of logic (and it was Aristotle himself who insisted that it was only the appearance of logic that mattered: it didn't have to be real scientific logic).

Aristotle said great communication requires ethos, pathos and logos

And that is right, isn't it? Because ethos, pathos and logos answer the three perennial questions that are buzzing around the minds of any group of people who are weighing up a potential leader: namely, 'Can I trust you?' (ethos); 'Do I care about what you are saying?' (pathos); and 'Are you right, or do you sound right?' (logos).

Great leaders need each of these three questions to be answered with a resounding 'yes'. It's like three cherries on the fruit machine. Getting just one right is not enough. You can't make an appeal purely on the basis of character or purely on the basis of emotion. You need all three to be present.

It is a three-legged stool: if one of them fails, the others collapse. If people don't trust a leader (no ethos), they won't care about their argument (no pathos) and they'll doubt its veracity (no logos). Likewise, if they don't care what the leader is saying (pathos), they will distrust their character (ethos) and won't bother listening to the argument (logos). And if someone says something plainly wrong (logos), then this casts doubt over their integrity (ethos) and will cause emotional shutdown (pathos).

Aristotle's rhetoric gives us an instant insight into the problem with most modern communication. All of the focus goes into getting the logic right, without regard to character or emotion. In fact, we are actively taught to banish these elements – we are told it is unprofessional to show emotion and too egotistical to talk about oneself. But these two elements are, as Aristotle said, essential, and they sit at the heart of the current crisis of leadership.

Just one in five people trust business and political leaders to tell the truth.[2] Only 13% of people are engaged at work.[3] People now spend more time online than they do with real people.[4]

A revival in rhetoric could help tackle this current crisis. I make this claim not because I'm a big fan of all things ancient, but because new developments in behavioural economics and neuroscience are proving that Aristotle's theories were astonishingly accurate.

Ancient rhetoric meets modern neuroscience

So now, if you don't mind, I'll lift you out of that ancient Greek taverna – yes, by all means, grab a couple of olives for the journey if you must – and whizz you forward to Parma, Italy, in 1994. We're in a cutting-edge laboratory full of brain scanners and computers. Amidst them stands a kindly faced, silver-haired Italian neuroscientist called Giacomo Rizzolatti who looks exactly like a scientist should look: white coat, a bit spinny-eyed, not unlike Doc from *Back to the Future*. But Rizzolatti is no crackpot, he is one of the world's greatest neuroscientists. Today, he is looking at motor co-ordination: observing a monkey's brain activity as the monkey scratches his arms and chews on his nuts (now, there's a sentence you must take care to get the right way around).

It is a hot day... Rizzolatti goes over to the fridge, grabs an ice cream and takes a bite. As he does so, the scanner jumps. Hmm. Rizzolatti turns around. He looks at the reading. It shows activity in the part of the monkey's brain associated with eating. He licks the ice cream again. Once more, the scanner leaps. He tries it a few more times. Each time, the response is repeated. Rizzolatti pauses. How extraordinary. Even though the monkey is absolutely static, it is clear his brain is imagining that it is he who is eating the ice cream at the same time as Rizzolatti. The monkey is mirroring him.

This was a momentous event. It represented the kind of profound scientific breakthrough that takes place only once every 50 years: indeed, Rizzolatti's discovery has been put up there along with the discovery of DNA. The insight that emerged that day was this: when people see someone acting with purpose, they mirror in their minds what the other person is doing. Their brains respond as if they were performing the task themselves.

This led to a new term – 'mirror neurons'. These neurons provided the answer to all sorts of previously inexplicable phenomena, from why we wince if we see someone hit their finger with a hammer, to why we feel such disappointment if we see someone miss a bus, to why it was that following the death of Diana, millions of people went out and bought that really appalling version of 'Candle in the Wind'. Once you know about mirror neurons you'll see them everywhere: from the way crowds hurry along and slow down collectively to how one person yawning at a dinner party makes everyone else yawn. It all comes down to mirror neurons.

Since then, billions of pounds have been invested in neuroscience. It is the new rock 'n' roll. We have neurosales, neuromarketing and before long the

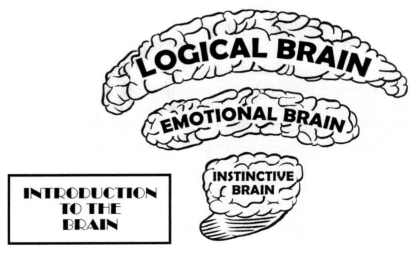

FIGURE 1.1 / Introduction to the brain

neuromantics will probably make a comeback – good news
for Spandau Ballet. But the point is that neuroscience has
provided unprecedented insight into the inner work-
ings of the brain. This means that great questions
that were once the subject of speculation can
now be answered with scientific certainty.

Now, I'm not a neuroscientist, I am a speechwriter,
but I have been struck by how closely neuroscience links
to ancient rhetoric. Aristotle's big three link perfectly to the big three
parts of the brain: the instinctive brain, the emotional brain and the logical brain.

Let's take a deeper look inside the brain and see (Figure 1.1).

The instinctive brain

The instinctive brain sits at the base of the brain. It can also be called the
intuitive brain, the unconscious brain or the reptilian brain… It is the oldest part of the brain, dating back 5 million years, and it is very impressive.
Not only is it incredibly busy (95% of brain activity takes place here), it is
also incredibly powerful, working at 80,000 times the speed of the logical
brain with no conscious effort at all on our part.

It's just as well it's so efficient because our survival depends on it: literally.
The operating mandate of the instinctive brain is to ensure our survival,
not just as individuals, but as a race and as a species. To that end, it has
supreme power to override every other part of our brain if it wants. That's
a good thing too. After all, what's more important than survival?

The instinctive brain ensures our survival in two ways. On the one hand,
through keeping our heart pumping, blood circulating, lungs breathing
and so on – we know about all that. But it also has another function
which is less well-known: the instinctive brain acts as a kind of internal
guardian angel. It operates an incredibly advanced CCTV detection system
with thousands of cameras spinning around every which way, constantly

taking pictures, processing them against past memories and then producing powerful impulses. These impulses instinctively draw us towards people and environments that it perceives to be safe and rewarding, whilst instinctively guiding us away from people and environments it perceives to be dangerous or threatening. Isn't that great?

Well... it would be seriously great, were it not for one flaw. The trouble is that, although the world around us has changed beyond all recognition in the last 5 million years, the instinctive brain has not. The instinctive brain still thinks we're Neanderthals prowling around on the savannah, when we're actually lying on the sofa snacking on Doritos, fiddling with our phones, watching TV.

Leaders speak to the instinctive brain's needs. They offer the promise of safety and rewards but, before we get to how we do that, let's step up, move on and have a nosey around the next level: the emotional brain.

The emotional brain

Now, simply using the word 'emotion' in a professional context can be enough to make some bristle. Emotion can still be considered a pejorative term – a 'women's issue', proving my earlier point about mankind still being basically Neanderthal. But emotion cannot be discounted in any analysis of leadership because you simply can't move people without emotion. The clue is in the word. 'E-motion': the word derives from the Greek – motion from within. Motion = movement.

There is a story about a guy who suffered a terrible car crash: a crash that left the emotional part of his brain irreparably damaged, whilst the logical part of his brain remained intact. Someone hatched the bright idea of sending him to Vegas, counting cards – as in *Rainman* – so they could all become rich. The trouble was, after he arrived in Vegas, they couldn't get him to do what they wanted. 'But we'll make lots of money!' 'So?' 'We'll make you rich!' 'So?' 'It's going to be fantastic.' 'So?' Without emotion, there is no motivational pull.

The emotional part of the brain is 20 times as powerful as the logical brain.[5] Emotions are overwhelming. We all know this. We can drown in emotion, and this is not some poetic metaphor, but a literal description of what happens. When we feel emotional, powerful drugs are released which flood our mind, be it oxytocin (the love/connection/cuddly drug), serotonin (the pride/esteem/confidence drug) or cortisol (the stress/fear/shock drug). The feelings induced by these drugs are so intoxicating, they reduce our capacity for logical thought. We love these drugs and crave them, and spend much of our time hunting them down, so desperate are we for the emotional fulfilment they provide.

Great leaders know this. They meet people's emotional needs. In return, they are given support. The American people felt afraid – George W. Bush made them feel safe. The British people felt anxious – Tony Blair gave them hope. People feel subdued and silenced – Russell Brand articulates their anger. There are heaps of emotions – 412 at the last count[6] – and great leaders know just how to tap into them.

I could talk for weeks about the different ways different leaders get different emotions going but there's not time: we still need to move up and look at the logical part of the brain. It would be rude to ignore the logical brain completely… particularly as it's so large.

The logical brain

The logical part of the brain represents 85% of its mass so it is by far the largest part of the brain. Relatively speaking, it is also the newest. It was the evolution of the logical brain that set the human race apart from our simian brothers, giving us our amazing powers to communicate, write music and invent: from the wheel to the printing press, antibiotics to the internet, the jet engine to the iPhone… Many have waxed lyrical about the amazing intelligence of the logical brain through the ages, from the ancient philosophers to the Enlightenment. But come closer and I'll tell you a secret. The logical brain is not actually half as clever as it's cracked up to be.

Just because the brain *can* be logical, doesn't mean it always *is* logical: to believe that would be to fall for that old fallacy of mistaking the specific for the general – the kind of thing a decent logical brain would have no problem sussing out, if only we had a half-decent logical brain that could draw such distinctions. We're not as clever as we think. As Aristotle said, it's not logic that is needed to prove a point, just the *appearance* of logic and anything, but anything, can *appear* logical.

The logical brain just does not have time to pause, scrutinize and test every piece of information that comes its way, weighing it up for truth and veracity; instead what it does is look for patterns, working largely on a rule-of-thumb basis. For instance, this person has told me the truth before, so they are probably telling me the truth now. That sounds right, so that probably is right. That sounds balanced, so it probably is balanced.

This is not to say the logical brain is a bit stupid. It's not. The logical brain is capable of the most extraordinary thinking – when we are completely calm, well fed and focused. It's just… well… how often does that happen? Right!

So, those are the three parts of the brain. Those are the parts of the brain we need to win over. This book is divided into three parts to reflect those three parts of the brain. Let's have a quick look at what lies ahead.

Winning the instinctive mind

The first part of the book looks at how leaders win over the instinctive mind. As I mentioned, the instinctive brain has two prime needs that must be met: avoid danger and find rewards. Leaders meet these needs.

This means the leader must be seen as friend, not foe. People instinctively determine whether someone is good or bad.[7] It's a snap judgement, happening almost instantaneously: Princeton University has it down at one-tenth of a second.[8] And it happens without any conscious intervention.

Everyone likes to claim that they are non-judgemental and free from prejudice, but this is wrong. It's the way we're designed and it's to protect us from danger. There's a tower of research on this point. You've probably already read before how juries make up their minds about a witness's credibility before they've even opened their mouth? There's much more besides this. Did you know people are more likely to trust someone who has a narrow face and brown eyes?[9] Did you know people are more likely to trust someone who has a baby face?[10] Did you know people are more likely to trust people who resemble themselves?[11] There was one study in which a group was shown photos of candidates in an election: they were able to predict with 70% accuracy which candidate won that election, based on nothing more than their photograph.[12]

These instinctive judgements do not happen randomly. What happens is that the instinctive mind rapidly checks images against a stored database of memories, as if it's flicking through old photo albums, looking for connections. If you look like a good face from the past, you pass the test. If you look like a bad face from the past, you fail. It's a super-fast process and it's a process leaders must win.

So what can leaders do to ensure they come up trumps? Obviously, we can't change our faces (unless you're reading this book in Los Angeles, in which case, yes, of course, you can change your face), but there are still some things we can do to improve our chances.

The starting point is that how we feel affects how others feel. If we feel anxious, we make others feel anxious. If we feel great, we make others feel great. It all comes back to those mirror neurons I mentioned at the beginning of this chapter. It never ceases to amaze me how some leaders speak as if they are dead on the inside and then berate those around them for being so unenergetic. If you want to enthuse people, then you must at the very least be enthused yourself. With full-frontal enthusiasm, there is just a small chance of winning people over; with no enthusiasm at all, there's no chance.

Breathing is also critical in leading the mood. Don't worry, I'm not going to turn all yogic and transcendental at this early stage in our relationship, but the simple insight here is this: we are sensitive to one another's breathing patterns. Are leaders breathing deeply or shallowly? This communicates two things of profound importance to the instinctive brain: first, is this person healthy enough to be our leader; and, second, is the environment we are in safe?

When David Cameron speaks, he often speaks in sharp, shallow sentences: his average sentence is just 13 words.[13] This is shorter than any other current-serving major politician in the UK and almost one-third of the length of the more long-winded politicians (William Hague's average sentence clocks in at 40 words long). This makes Cameron sound breathless: 'Broken Homes. Failing Schools. Sink Estates.'

When he speaks like this, he is using an ancient Roman rhetorical device called asyndeton. Short, sharp sentences. If a speaker speaks urgently, disconnectedly, like that, it sounds as if they are hyperventilating. This suggests fear. And that fear transfers. So, if you run a focus group on David Cameron, you'll find a common reaction is angst: he makes people feel ill at ease. Some describe him as shrill. His breathing moulds these impressions. And, by the way, I'm not saying his approach is necessarily wrong. Some leaders deliberately set out to create anxiety with short sentences and that can, in some circumstances, be perfectly valid – after all, Bob Geldof's 'Give us your fucking money' statement on TV in the middle of Live Aid didn't fare so badly. And, as long as that's the strategy, fine.

But now compare Cameron to Obama. Barack Obama: my lord, can that man breathe. He breathes so deeply that some of his sentences can run to 140 words and beyond and, when you combine this extraordinary flow in his sentences with his uniquely rich, sonorous tone, you can see how he imbues in people this deep, irresistible sense of calm so they wouldn't mind if he just carried on talking forever and ever and ever... I heard Obama on the radio the other day speaking about Ebola, a deadly disease that has claimed thousands of lives. Yet despite the terrifying content of his words, he did not leave me feeling in the slightest bit panicky or agitated. I felt that, no matter how dastardly the threats facing the world, at least the right guy is in charge. That's the Language of Leadership. He feels calm. His supporters feel calm. His confidence transfers.

It's the same with smiling. If you've ever had the pleasure of observing any truly great leader in action – Bill Clinton, Tony Blair, Nelson Mandela, Richard Branson, Steve Jobs – you must have noticed how their huge grins stretched from ear to ear. These are genuine, heartfelt, authentic smiles: not contrived contortions. Smiling is so damn simple. It is the quickest win imaginable for wannabe leaders yet still so many fail at this first post by looking glum. Who wants to be a part of that? You can't sell gloom. We see someone smiling and people's instinctive reaction is 'I want what they're on!'

The other aspect that speaks to the instinctive mind is metaphor. Hardly anyone ever talks about metaphor. There are certain mantras about business communication: always write in the active, never try to put more than one idea in each sentence and always choose simple words over long words. These are all simple enough, easy to put into practice but, for my money, if you want *real* power and leadership, you have to understand metaphor. Metaphors provide the images that stick. See? *Stick*.

Metaphors are everywhere: from everyday conversations to newspaper headlines to the titles of books: *Blink, Tipping Point, Nudge*. On average, we use six metaphors a minute.[14] The choice of metaphor often proves decisive in whether an argument is won or lost. Research has shown how changing nothing more than the metaphor in a piece of text can lead to profoundly different reactions to questions as varied as whether or not to back a foreign war, whether a share price appears likely to go up or down or what should be done locally to tackle crime. One thing that makes metaphors so powerful is that, half the time, people don't even realize a metaphor is being used.

Let me give you an example: 'The Arab Spring'. Chances are you've never paused to consider whether that is a metaphor, but it is, so let's take a minute to explore it, shall we? So, the Arab Spring... Mmmmm... Doesn't that sound lovely? Birds singing... Warm sunshine... Buds opening... Flowers blooming... Beautiful. A time of renewal, rejuvenation and rebirth. But yet, hang on a cotton-picking minute, what we're talking about here is complete carnage, isn't it? It's an endless series of terrible revolutions, bloody civil wars and leaders being savagely toppled and in some cases brutally executed. Any rational analysis shows it's a disaster – even the most optimistic experts suggest it will take decades to resolve – yet the public is not only sanguine about all this, they are palpably supportive.

Polls show that a clear majority of people regard the Arab Spring as a positive process.[15] The metaphor is critical in leading opinion. Spring speaks directly to the instinctive mind. It plants an image of nature: a scenario in which the best option is inaction: just sit back and let nature take its course and everything will be alright. Now, had a different metaphor been used – the *tsunami* of change, the Arab *furnace*, the North African *disease* – people would have demanded action because that's the natural response to those metaphors. Tsunamis need clean-up operations, fires must be extinguished and diseases have to be cured.

As a leader, you must understand the power of your metaphors: it's not just about finding the metaphors that can help, it's also about avoiding ones that will hinder.

I'll give you an example. Many leaders speak using the metaphor of the car – they talk about *driving* change, *accelerating* reform and *firing* on all cylinders. These metaphors are endemic in business, politics and public services. They are the metaphors of management consultancies. Leaders find this metaphor appealing: after all, if their companies are cars, then they must be the drivers: in charge and in control. Great. So, if they want the company to move, all they have to do is switch the ignition, put their foot down and vroom vroom – away they go. That's why leaders like this metaphor: it reinforces their desired self-image as omnipotent and omniscient.

But this metaphor is appalling for those on the receiving end. For if the leader is the driver and the organisation is a car, then that makes the people within it nuts and bolts, so not there to innovate or create, simply to fulfil a function: no more, no less; and as soon as they fail to fulfil that function, then be in no doubt they will be extracted and disposed of instantly. So when leaders use the car metaphor, it might make them feel more powerful, but it leaves the people they're addressing feeling dejected, dispirited and depressed. Of course, when surveys are carried out people will never say 'I didn't like their metaphor', but their response will discreetly demonstrate how the metaphor snaked into their mind and brought them down. They might sarcastically murmur 'Full steam ahead, then!' They may say they feel 'ground down'... Harsh words, but hardly surprising if their instinctive mind visualises them as part of a car: that is, after all, what happens to nuts and bolts – they get ground down.

The Language of Leadership guides us away from such metaphors towards metaphors that are more natural and timeless. The test is: would this metaphor have worked 30,000 years ago? If the answer is yes, it's probably going to work on the instinctive brain today. So we place a premium on people, sustenance, climate, food and nature metaphors.

People metaphors cultivate intimacy and affection. And when we use action language within a metaphorical frame of personification (e.g. 'reaching out', 'getting a grip', 'kicking into action'), functional magnetic resonance imaging (fMRI) scanners show that we light up the parts of people's brains that would be activated if they were performing those tasks themselves: so the leader who personifies the company can achieve a kind of osmosis between themselves and their employees... That is the Language of Leadership. That is how leaders can really get into people's heads – literally.

Fascinating, isn't it? More later – I promise. We must move on. Let's go up a level and look at how we get the emotions going.

Winning the emotional mind

The emotional brain is like a big pharmacy, full of vats of cortisol, serotonin, oxytocin and dopamine that we are desperate to break into because we love the powerful feelings that those drugs create (Figure 1.2). A large chunk of people's lives is spent chasing the emotional high provided by these drugs – whether that's through watching films, checking Facebook,

FIGURE 1.2 / The pharmacy

going on roller-coasters or anything else. We love the highs, we love the lows, we love the feelings. Great leaders know how to get these drugs flowing. I mentioned Boris Johnson in the Introduction, but different leaders use a number of different techniques which we will explore throughout Part II of this book.

Repetition is one way to get the emotional juices going. Repetition is an ancient Roman rhetorical device: known back in the day as anaphora. Anaphora has featured as the centrepiece of some of the most famous speeches in history, from Churchill's 'We shall fight them on the beaches' to Martin Luther King's 'I have a dream'. The repetition had an extraordinary effect. The pattern, the pull and the predictability can make people high.

Another way that leaders get the drugs flowing is through praise. Praise causes serotonin to be released, which makes people feel calm and confident. It might not surprise you to know that calm, confident people perform better than people who are stressed and irritable – this is generally good news. Why so many leaders imagine that lording it around is a good idea, who knows? It's praise that promotes high performance. And praise is not just good for the person on the receiving end: it also makes the person who is doing the praising feel great. Research shows that, during praise, serotonin levels rise both in the brains of the person being praised and the person praising. This unites them, creating a safe, supportive, comfortable environment, making everyone feel great.

One of the other ways to stir up people's emotions is through a good old-fashioned story. A good story, well told, can cause three different hormones to squirt in the brain. As we talk about the feelings and character of the protagonist, oxytocin, the connection hormone is released (as we see the world through the eyes of the protagonist). As the critical dilemma of the story is set out (every story needs a dilemma at its heart: a conflict awaiting resolution), cortisol, the stress hormone is released. As the story is resolved, dopamine, the reward drug, is produced (giving us that beautiful sense of satisfaction we get when all the pieces suddenly fit together).

There was one piece of research in which a group of people were shown a little animated story about a young boy and his father coping with the news that the little boy had just been diagnosed with cancer and given months to live. After the film, the audience was asked to give money. Their levels of generosity were directly proportionate to the amount of cortisol and oxytocin that had been produced in their brain. Those who had no cortisol or oxytocin gave no money. Those who had low cortisol and oxytocin levels gave less money. Those who had high cortisol and oxytocin levels gave more money. So, if leaders are looking to change behaviour, these are the drugs we have to release.[16]

Great leaders are often great storytellers. Stories can elevate the mundane to the sublime. The story might come from history – a quick reference to Gandhi or Mandela can spark all sorts of emotions – or it might be personal. It doesn't matter. In the Language of Leadership, what matters is how we make people feel.

But enough on emotion. Onward and upward. Shall we take a look at logic?

Winning the logical mind

Part III of this book is about how we can win over the logical mind. As I've already said, this is not about establishing pure logic or ensuring that your strategy is totally right: I'm assuming you've done all that. My concern is with language: making sure that you sound right.

Neuroscientists have shown that when we hear people speak, the words go to two different parts of our brain: one part analyses the meaning of what is being said, the other analyses the music.[17] So, for leaders, it's not enough to make sure the substance of our argument is right, we must also be concerned with the style. It's not just about the meaning, it's about the music. It's not just about the reasoning, it's about the rhythm.

There. Sounded nice, didn't it? That's because that little sentence used three Language of Leadership techniques: alliteration, balance and the rule of three, all of which play a critical role in great modern communication, but all of which date back to ancient rhetoric.

I'll never forget, soon after I met my wife, Lucy, we went for dinner at her uncle's house. Lucy's uncle is a classicist. When he found out I was a speechwriter he was very interested and said, 'Oh, do you use tricolon then?' I didn't have a clue what he was talking about. At first, I thought he was enquiring after my digestion. He explained: tricolon is an ancient Roman rhetorical device. It is also known as the rule of three. When we present arguments in threes it creates the illusion of completeness, certainty and conviction.

This sounded ludicrous, but he then reeled off a whole series of examples: from politics ('Government of the people, by the people, for the people', 'Education! Education! Education!', 'No! No! No!'), film (*The Good, the Bad and the Ugly*, 'Infamy, Infamy, they've all got it in for me', *Sex, Lies and Videotape*) and advertising ('A Mars a day helps you work, rest and play', 'Beanz Meanz Heinz', 'Snap! Crackle! Pop!'). I was gobsmacked. Amazed. So simple, yet so powerful. And it had to be threes. One less and the argument lacked force and impact. One more and it sounded over-egged, unbalanced, hyperbolic and even a little bit bonkers.

This was a revelation. I felt I'd rumbled one of the biggest secrets of the English language. And it's not just a theory or some ancient rhetorical relic: we now know it works. Research at Georgetown University and the University of California in 2014 put the rule of three to the test. They compared the effectiveness of three-part lists and four-part lists in persuasion,[18] testing them in all kinds of scenarios. In each case, the three-part list fared better than the four-part. So, a product should be 'faster, better, cheaper' – not 'faster, better, cheaper and prettier'. A policy initiative should be 'socially, economically and environmentally sustainable' – not 'socially, economically, environmentally and politically sustainable'. If you're interested in reading the research, Google it: it's very readable. The research is called, 'Three Charms, Four Alarms'.

'What?!' I hear you cry, 'So, there they were, telling everyone to use the rule of three but then they didn't use the rule of three in their own title?' Well, yes. That's right. But that is absolutely fine because there's separate research that shows people are more likely to believe something is true if it rhymes, than if it doesn't rhyme. Crazy, isn't it? Crazy, but true. So… 'A quick rhyme saves time'. 'To sound sublime, try rhyme'. Or 'Rhymey? Blimey!'

Rhymes have had persuasive qualities since the dawn of time. Rhymes feature in many ancient aphorisms. That is why Shakespeare talked about 'rhyme and reason': it can be easy to confuse the two. Rhymes are considered to be signifiers of truth, but, of course, there is no reason why a statement should be any more likely to be true simply because it rhymes. In fact, the opposite is often the case: rhymes can be very effective in concealing fallacies. An apple a day doesn't really keep the doctor away: if only that were true – the health service would save a fortune. Perhaps you remember the killer line from the OJ Simpson trial – 'if the glove don't fit, you must acquit'. And then there is the famous 'i before e except after c' – a rule that is still drummed into every schoolchild from the second they can pick up a pen, even though it is complete tosh.

I wrote speeches for Alan Johnson when he was Britain's Education Secretary. When we were at the Department for Education, formal guidance was sent to each of the 24,000 schools in England and Wales imploring them to stop teaching the 'i before e' rule because it's simply not true. There are about 50 examples of words in which the rule is right but around 900 examples of words in which it is not. And yet the rhyme persists, even though it is an*cie*nt, defi*cie*nt and has no basis in s*cie*nce (see what I did there?).

Many people say, 'Ah, yes – rhymes might work on some people, but they'd *never* work on me. And they'd never work in my profession.' That's what everyone says. The research tracked that too: even people who have been convinced by rhyme vehemently deny that the rhyme influenced them. No one is too smart to be above this kind of deception. Don't forget: the example I started with – three charms, four alarms – came from two of the greatest universities in the world. It's not deception: it's about making sure the style supports the substance. I once explained this on one of my Language of Leadership workshops and someone from a commercial bank said, 'Oh yes! Like "You've got to speculate to accumulate".' 'Exactly!' I replied. Perhaps the whole financial crisis was predicated on a rhyming fallacy. Maybe it could have been averted if people had instead been saying 'Speculation leads to liquidation'.

The Language of Leadership is not concerned only with the sounds of sentences but also the structures. If you're a fan of *The West Wing,* you might remember an episode called 'Post Hoc, Ergo Propter Hoc'. This rather fancy Latin term means 'after this, therefore because of this'. The fallacy here is this: when two sentences are placed next to one another, people assume a causal connection between the two.

The other day, I was sitting in the Blue Boar, a famous Westminster watering hole, and the Conservative Party chairman, Grant Shapps, was sitting on the table next to me speaking with some journalists. I couldn't resist earwigging and at one point he said, 'We have cut spending on police and local authorities and satisfaction in both has gone up.' This was a clever line. He was suggesting a causal link between cuts and satisfaction without explicitly asserting it. A cut-and-shut of the two ideas simply leads the listener to conclude that. *Post hoc ergo propter hoc* is a great way to imply credit without positively making the assertion. It can feature in all sorts of scenarios: 'We closed down the HR team, profits have gone up by 80%.'

People fall for *post hoc ergo propter hoc* all the time. When I was younger, I used to go to the gym a bit. I remember once, a relatively successful amateur boxer told me he'd heard that Mike Tyson used to soak his hands in horse urine the day before every fight. He was now applying the same technique. *Post hoc ergo propter hoc*. Personally, I imagine other factors were more critical to Mike Tyson's success, but I wasn't going to say that to old pissy-hands. He was bigger than me.

The Language of Leadership

So there are the three parts of the brain that the leader must win over. In terms of *how* we win them over, well, this is where the Language of Leadership turns modern communication on its head. Most modern communication starts and ends with logic, which is why it fails. The Language of Leadership starts with instinct, because that is how the brain works.

Most modern communication starts and ends with logic, which is why it fails

The thing is that we are fundamentally instinctive creatures. Think about a typical day – the way we shop, the way we drive, the way we walk. Most of the time, we're not thinking about what we do. We're acting from habits, rituals and impulses. Our instinctive mind is like the Pied Piper that our body automatically follows. We are led by our instincts. This is true, not just about the day-to-day stuff, but also about some of the most critical decisions in our lives, including who we marry, who our best friends are, where we live and where we work. 'We clicked.' 'We knew in our gut it was the house for us as soon as we walked in.' 'It felt right…' These expressions all point to the instinctive brain's primacy. We do not start with logic. Far from it. We start with instinct. In truth, most of the time we only use our logical brain to construct a relatively decent logical-ish-sounding argument to justify the instinctive judgement we made earlier. So, we might instinctively like the look of a house: then we set our logical mind to work proving that this is the right house for us to buy. We selectively pick any information about schools, facilities and crime rates that supports our instinctive mind whilst conveniently ignoring anything that might prove us wrong.

That is why the Language of Leadership starts with instinct: because the brain starts with instinct. Neuroscientists have a model they call 'APET' (Figure 1.3).[19] Whilst I'm simplifying this, as I'm simplifying a lot of complicated neuroscience in this book (on the basis that it would bore you silly if I explained everything in detail), this shows that external stimuli travel through the brain in this order: first, instinctive brain; second, emotional brain; finally, logical brain.

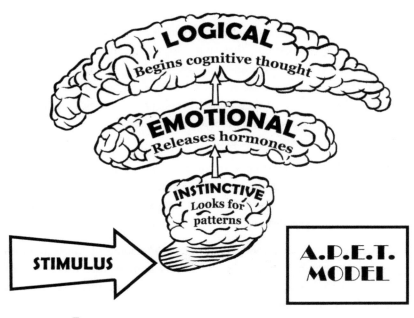

FIGURE 1.3 / The APET model

So how does this work in practice? Say you are walking down the street and someone comes towards you, hand outstretched as if to shake your hand. First, your instinctive brain processes this picture against past experiences and makes a rapid judgement on whether or not you're safe. Your emotional brain then squirts out an emotional chemical response – be it cortisol in case of fear or oxytocin in case of connection. Finally, your logical mind kicks into action, and considers rationally whether or not you want to stop and chat.

The brain process is identical whoever goes through this experience. However, different brains generate different responses. Some people might be happy to see someone friendly in the street, others might fear they are about to get mugged. It depends on their life experiences. It's as if a car backfires. To most people, that's no big deal. Yet if there is someone nearby who has recently returned from service in Afghanistan, they might have a completely different response.

That's what happens in a chance encounter on the street, but the same brain process also occurs when leaders are first introduced. And the truth is that most leaders fail right at the outset. They fail the blink test. They might look vaguely nervous, they might look miserable, they might look like they don't care. For someone purporting to be a leader, this represents a threat. Many leaders arouse completely the wrong emotions. Ask your friends and families what they think of the leaders in their lives. It rarely takes more than 30 seconds before you start hearing expressions of frustration, disappointment and anger.

The Language of Leadership turns this around. It is based upon great leaders progressively winning over the instinctive, emotional and logical mind – in that order. Figure 1.4 sets out the range of techniques you can use to win over those different parts of the brain.

I appreciate that at this point you'll understand some of the techniques in Figure 1.4 but not others. So, to quickly demonstrate the power of the Language of Leadership model, let me show you how this works in practice by constructing communication ladders out of the techniques in the diagram. This is not to suggest that communication should be quite

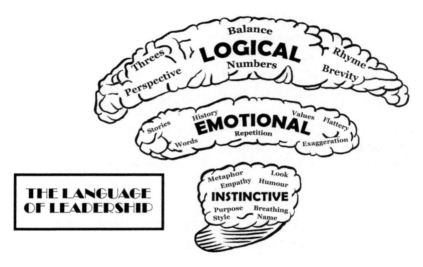

FIGURE 1.4 / The Language of Leadership

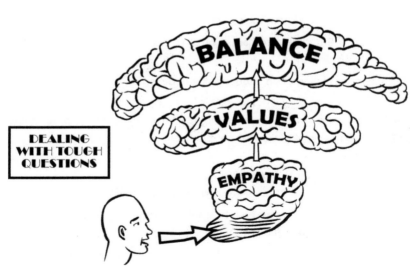

FIGURE 1.5 / Dealing with tough questions

so formulaic, it is just to illustrate the effectiveness of starting with the instinctive brain and working upwards.

Sequence one – dealing with difficult questions

How about this one? Empathy – Values – Balance.

So let's try it in this scenario: a politician is on the BBC's *Question Time*, responding to an angry woman whose husband has been subjected to some shabby treatment by the National Health Service (NHS):

> *Empathy* – I understand you're angry.
>
> *Values* – But we all want the best for the National Health Service.
>
> *Balance* – That's why we've promised not just to match government spending on the NHS but to increase it by 5% every year.

Hmm. Not bad. Let's check it in another scenario: a chief executive officer (CEO) responding to mounting staff anger after announcing a pay freeze:

> *Empathy* – I know you wanted more. Were it down to me alone, I'd have paid you more. I know you're worth that.
>
> *Values* – But times are hard. We can't pay more than we earn. That would be disastrous.
>
> *Balance* – I know this is a tough thing to do, but it's the right thing to do.

Okay. Let's raise the stakes even higher. Let's try it on a homophobic preacher addressing a gay rights conference:

> *Empathy* – I understand you find my views abhorrent. I understand some of you think I should not even have been invited here today.
>
> *Values* – But by coming here to speak, I am showing you respect. Can't you show me the same?
>
> *Balance* – What value is a right to express our sexuality if we do not also have a right to speak...

Well, it might not have them cheering in the aisles but it might at least get him out alive.

That's just one communication ladder. We could try out all sorts of others.

So, how about Humour – Story – Brevity – to open up a conference speech?

Would Purpose – Values – Rule of Three – be a good way to begin an inspirational talk?

How about Breathlessness – Exaggeration – Number – for starting off a big product launch?

The possibilities are limitless. The most important thing is that you win over the instinctive and emotional brain before even trying to come in with the logic. These are the bits that so many leaders ignore and it is that which leads to their downfall. Winning over the whole brain, not just one part of the brain, is what gives leaders who speak the Language of Leadership the edge.

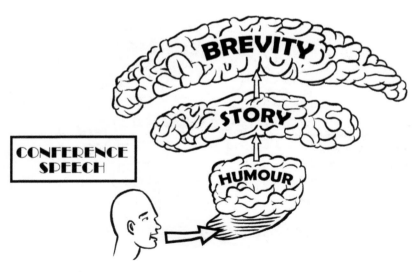

FIGURE 1.6 The conference speech

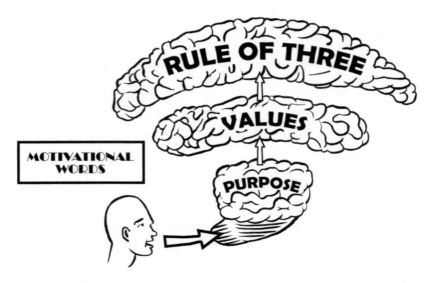

FIGURE 1.7 / Motivational words

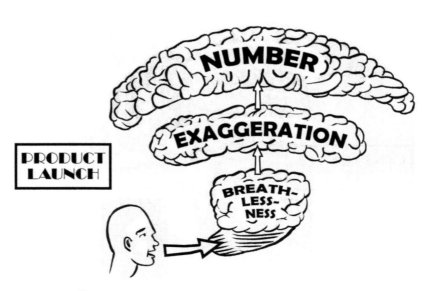

FIGURE 1.8 / The product launch

Sequence two: making persuasive speeches

Right, let's raise our ambition. Let's try running two communication ladders in sequence, using six devices in total. Let's see if we can use this formula to create a quick, punchy, self-contained speech.

The first device is breathlessness. Short, jagged sentences. Like Cameron. Speaks to the instinctive. Communicates danger.

The second device is repetition. Repetition shows emotion. Repetition shows passion. Repetition shows conviction.

The third device is balance: suggesting our ideas are not bonkers, but balanced; not madness, but measured; not lunacy, but logical.

The fourth device is metaphor, when we plant the seed of an idea but don't let it grow out of control because we must save room for the next device.

The fifth device is exaggeration. The best thing ever. It sweeps people off their feet. Every time.

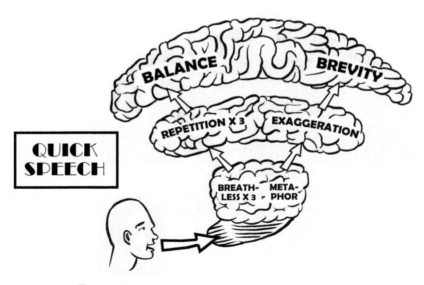

FIGURE 1.9 / The quick speech

And then end with brevity. Just like that.

So, let's try out these two ladders in sequence, making a case for something that no one can possibly disagree with (unless you're allergic!)... the joy of nuts:

> *Cashews. Pistachios. Hazelnuts.*
>
> *Nuts are great sprinkled on thick chocolate desserts.*
>
> *Nuts are great by the fire at Christmas.*
>
> *Nuts are great to snack on during a good film.*
>
> *It's not just the taste I love, it's the whole experience...*
>
> *They're orgasmic!*
>
> *It sends shivers from my head to my toes.*
>
> *So don't go nuts, eat nuts.*

This is pretty effective: because it appeals to each part of the mind in turn, it has a natural story arc. It works. But, equally, the same structure can be used to argue the polar opposite view:

> *The case against nuts:*
>
> *Full of oil. High in fat. Laced with salt.*
>
> *Nuts are terrible for our health.*
>
> *Nuts are terrible for the NHS.*
>
> *Nuts are terrible for society.*
>
> *They look small but their impact is huge.*
>
> *Silent killers lurking in society's shadows.*
>
> *We start thinking we'll just have one, then we say just one more... Before we know it we are stuffing our face full and we can't stop.*
>
> *Just say no.*

This formula clearly works on trivial issues such as nuts – now let's try it on a bigger issue: something that really matters, such as climate change. This is an issue, after all, where action is needed.

Let's start by making a call for the world to act:

> The world has not done enough on climate change:
>
> *Flooding in London. Droughts in Africa. Freak snowstorms in New York.*
>
> *Yet still there are some people saying there is no such thing as climate change.*
>
> *Still there are some people trying to discredit the scientists who are working so hard to combat this.*
>
> *Still there are some people preaching business as usual.*
>
> *Climate change is not some distant threat, it is here.*
>
> *We can't bury our heads in the sand any more.*
>
> *This is the biggest threat facing humanity. If we don't fight it, no one will. There has never been a better time to act.*
>
> *Let's go for it!*

Okay. Now, let's switch it around and try the opposite tack:

> The world has seized the initiative in tackling climate change:
>
> *New green taxes. Innovative markets in carbon. Massive investment in renewables.*
>
> *The whole planet agrees that climate change is happening.*
>
> *The whole planet accepts that climate change has been caused by man.*
>
> *And the whole planet is now pulling together to tackle this issue.*
>
> *Instead of criticizing and carping about what hasn't been done, we should pull together and praise the progress that has been achieved.*
>
> *We know there's still a long way to go.*
>
> *But if we push too hard, too fast, there's a danger the global consensus will shatter.*
>
> *Then it's game over.*

These are just illustrative examples. The possibilities are endless. The critical starting point is winning over the instinctive brain. So let's start by looking closer at this fascinating part of the human mind.

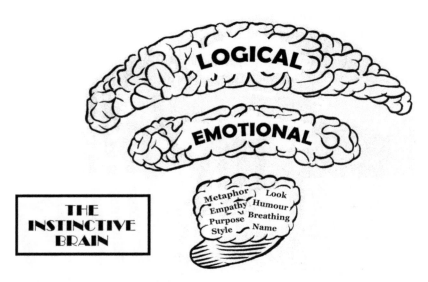

part I

Winning the Instinctive Mind

FIGURE PT I.1 / The instinctive brain

'I will not attempt any definition of instinct.'
Charles Darwin, *The Origin of Species*

'Instinct leads, intelligence does but follow.'
William James, 1902

Instinctive mind as survival system

Imagine... you are walking across the top of a mountain, completely naked, wet grass beneath your feet, the wind whistling in your ears. Down below, you hear the sound of a stream cascading and you smile. You instinctively know the valley is filled with forest fruits at this time of year and, although you have already walked miles, the closer you get, the more energized you feel. The vision of ripe blackberries and fresh water grows in your mind. Then, suddenly, there's a sound. A branch snaps. You stop dead. Paralysed. Filled with fear. Suddenly, a wild beast tears out of the forest, eyes dilated, teeth bared. It's coming right at you. *What do you do now*?

This is the world we faced 5 million years ago. It's a hunter-gatherer world: a world in which every day is a fight for survival. This is the world for which our instinctive mind was designed to cope.

The instinctive brain has two supreme instructions: minimise danger and maximise rewards.[1] Our whole body is designed instinctively to obey these

FIGURE PT I.2 / **The instinctive leader**

instructions without question. When there is any perception of danger, we are highly motivated to address that danger: cortisol and adrenalin are pumped out to make us focus and to sharpen our powers. Where there is any prospect of reward, we are highly motivated to obtain that reward: the brain squirts out increasing quantities of dopamine to entice us closer and closer to our reward.

These processes were designed beautifully for the world of 5 million years ago. The trouble is that, whilst the world has changed beyond all recognition since then, the instinctive mind remains basically the same.

Today's great leaders would have been great leaders 5 million years ago. They meet the instinctive brain's need to minimise danger and maximise reward. They offer the promise of safety and reward. Let's look at this more closely.

The leader promises safety

People decide in one-tenth of a second whether or not to trust a leader. As the instinctive brain's internal CCTV cameras quickly check someone up and down, there is one part of the body that is particularly important: the 2.5 inches between mouth and eyebrows. The brain has a special area devoted to facial recognition, which is incredibly good at interpreting and understanding what is going on in this region. And the instinctive mind is astonishingly accomplished: it can see things the naked eye would never spot.

People decide in one-tenth of a second whether or not to trust a leader

For instance, the instinctive brain just *knows* whether or not a smile is genuine. You could never consciously identify the 14 muscle movements that make a smile genuine. But your instinctive mind can instantly spot that tell-tale contraction of the zygomatic major muscle and contraction of the orbicularis oculi to let you know: this informs your judgement as to whether or not they're safe.

Likewise, the eyes. Eyes are the windows to the soul, as Shakespeare put it, and the instinctive brain can see the most extraordinary things therein.

Some research was carried out where men were shown pictures of women and asked to rate their attractiveness. The men were consistently attracted to the women with the most dilated eyes. As it happens, when women are sexually aroused, their eyes naturally dilate. They can't help it. But the men swore that they hadn't noticed their eyes were dilated. They also swore that they didn't know that dilated eyes were a sign of sexual arousal. So their rational brains didn't have a clue what was going on but the instinctive mind was doing all the hard work, basically selecting and guiding them towards those with whom they stood the best chance of having sex.[2]

Eyes can unwittingly reveal sexual arousal, but they can also reveal when someone is feeling hostile. This helps people avoid leaders who might represent a threat. But it is a risk for any leader who is feeling cross. So great leaders must avoid this. One leader I work with has a neat approach: whenever he has a potentially confrontational meeting, instead of doing a 'face to face' he does a 'walk and talk'. He takes people for a stroll through nearby Kensington Gardens. This spares people the feeling of being 'eye-balled'. It also has other positive effects: the exercise gets the endorphins flowing and the literal journey supports the metaphorical journey. Win win win.

The walk and talk was made famous as a piece of fiction in the TV series *The West Wing* but it was a technique used in real life by Steve Jobs. Jim Gianopulos, CEO of Fox, has told how, when Apple was negotiating to find a new business model for selling films within iTunes, discussions reached stalemate. Gianopulos retreated to his holiday isle for time out and refused to take calls. In the end, Steve Jobs emailed him and suggested he would come out to his holiday isle so they could go for a walk on the beach. They resolved their differences, did an amazing deal on iTunes and the two went on to become great friends.[3]

Great leaders do not harass, they show humility. They do not intimidate, they embrace. They do not bully and bulldoze, they offer a warm, welcoming environment. The leader reaches out and says 'Come in. Join us. Feel the warmth.' It's an enticing draw. People are highly motivated to join groups. Since as far back in human history as we can trace, from the

African savannah to the Amazonian rainforest, humans have grouped in numbers of 50 to 150. Why? Safety. Lucy and I once camped in the Serengeti, sleeping in a tent with nothing more than canvas between us and the lions. We were safe because of the group. The lions would have been afraid to attack us because our group of tents was larger than their pride of lions. Our instinctive brains know that it keeps us safe. It's a powerful pull. Our need to belong is as basic to our survival as our need for food and oxygen.[4] That is why, having joined a group, people will do anything they can to stay in. And it is the leader who controls who is in and who is out. The group is everything: there's no 'you' and 'me', it's all about 'we'.

The leader promises reward

People are also instinctively drawn to leaders who offer the promise of reward. This is not about identifying people who have a big wad of money in their wallet, it is more about finding people who have that special X factor: the glint in the eye, that magic quality, charisma. I can sum this up in one word: purpose. People are drawn towards leaders with purpose. There is a clear survival reason why the instinctive brain should guide us towards people with purpose: it is people with purpose who take forward society, securing our supremacy, ensuring our survival.

There are two things that go on in the brain when we're with purposeful people. First, they start up our mirror neurons. It is only when we see people acting with purpose that our mirror neurons are activated, according to UCLA neuroscientist Dan Siegel.[5] In this way, mirror neurons can prove critical to leaders in shaping group behaviour: by getting people to copy. As the American philosopher Eric Hoffer once said, 'When people are free to do as they please, they usually imitate each other.'[6] This is a trait everyone is born with. Copying is not something we learn. One piece of research showed a baby copying her mother as she stuck out her tongue just 41 minutes after childbirth.[7] So copying must be instinctive.

Great leaders know this: they know that creating an enthused, committed, high-performing workforce requires them to be enthused, committed and high-performing leaders. They know it is their responsibility to lead behaviour, that behaviour doesn't change in isolation. Ever wondered why people screamed at The Beatles? Because The Beatles screamed at them. They started it. Mirror neurons.

The second thing that draws people to leaders with purpose is the allure of dopamine. Great leaders have a vision. By explaining their vision and purpose clearly, they activate the brain's reward system. This results in more and more dopamine being issued as that vision gets closer to realisation. The clearer the vision, the greater the flow of dopamine. If the vision is blurry, out of focus or unclear, the instinctive brain won't be bothered.

Images strike deep in the instinctive brain because the instinctive brain is primarily sensual. Once a powerful vision lodges in the brain, it is impossible to shift. If I say to you, 'Don't think of a big green elephant', what's in your mind now? And no matter how hard you try, you won't be able to budge that big green elephant. Or, if I say to you, 'Don't think of me now, as naked as the day I was born, holding a rifle in one hand and eating a bacon sandwich with the other', what's in your mind now? Sorry. I'm proving a point. The instinctive mind is a funny creature: not as sophisticated as we might hope. In particular, the instinctive is unable to distinguish between negative and positive imagery: they are equally powerful. This is why it is so futile when parents shout at their children, 'Don't touch the knife!' The first thing the child will want to do is grab the knife because that is the image in their mind's eye.[8]

Some smart leaders get around this and play it the other way, like when one of Obama's spokespeople said, 'I'm not saying it's morning in America.'[9] He planted a powerful image, even though he said he was not trying to make that connection. The image he planted was metaphorical. In the instinctive mind, the metaphorical is far more powerful than the literal. That is why metaphor is the first thing we're going to look at now. Metaphors will blow your mind. And, yes: that was indeed another metaphor.

Metaphors that Move Minds

'The greatest thing by far is to be a master of metaphor. It is the one thing that cannot be learned from others; it is also a sign of GENIUS, since a good metaphor implies an eye for resemblance.'

Aristotle

Leadership and imagery

The Dark Ages. The Enlightenment. The invisible hand of the market. The Industrial Revolution. The Iron Curtain. The wind of change. The Swinging Sixties. The Winter of Discontent. The Iron Lady. The financial storm. The credit crunch. The housing bubble. Nudge. Blink. Tipping point.

These are all metaphors. They say a picture is worth a thousand words. Well, this handful of metaphors has spawned hundreds of images which have spread across millions of minds. Metaphors pack enormous power into a tiny space. They plant ideas deep in the instinctive mind, where they take root and grow, spreading around, affecting the way people think, feel and act.

Metaphors plant ideas deep in the instinctive mind

Metaphors are a crucial element in the Language of Leadership. But let's start with the basics: what is a metaphor?

Metaphors

A metaphor is basically a substitution. When we use metaphor, we substitute one thing for something else. So, if we are thinking about this mathematically, the basic formula for a metaphor would be this: x=y.

Let me demonstrate: if I say to you, 'I'm at a crossroads', the x=y metaphor in that would be that my life = a journey. That is the image I plant: that image would then lead our conversation in particular ways, so you may well reuse that image in your response. You might ask: 'Which way are you going?' By establishing a particular image for our discussion, it makes you more likely to offer certain viewpoints, less likely to offer others.

There are lots of well-established examples of x=y. For instance, many people see ideas as containers (it's got *holes* in it, let's *unpack* that); arguments as wars (I'm keeping my *powder* dry, we *shot* down their argument); houses as people (it's got great *character*, the kitchen is the *heart* of the house). George Lakoff has written a lot about these different metaphors in his book, *Metaphors We Live By*.[1]

We use metaphor all the time: not just in poetry or high-flown rhetoric, but as part and parcel of everyday chit-chat. It is hard to speak for very long at all without resorting to some kind of metaphor. We use metaphors once every sixteen words on average. So our conversation is littered with metaphors. See? Like that. '*Littered*?' But is that an appropriate metaphor? Is that the image I want to plant? The x=y there is that metaphors = rubbish. That is not the image I want to plant: I want to convince you that metaphors are powerful.

We use metaphors once every sixteen words

So, let's try again. How about this: 'our conversation is *loaded* with metaphors'. Better? The x=y there is that metaphors = weapons… That's not bad. Certainly, that would fit within Lakoff's 'arguments = war metaphor', to which we can easily subscribe. But, personally, I'm not mad on war metaphors. Let's try another metaphor. How about this: 'we *scatter* metaphors all over the place'. Yes. I like that. The x=y there is that metaphors = seeds. That seems a good metaphor: the metaphor of ideas as seeds has been around for thousands of years. In fact, the very origin of the word propaganda comes from within that metaphorical frame – we *propagate* ideas. So… That'll do. That's the metaphor I'm going to use: the x=y will be metaphors = seeds.

In fact, I already used that metaphor at the beginning of this chapter, when I said metaphors '*plant* ideas *deep*, where they take *root* and *grow, spreading* wide'. You may not have noticed the metaphor at the time but that's what makes metaphors so potent. Most of the time, people don't even realize they're being used. And yet each time a metaphor is used, it leads people a particular way. That's the secret power of metaphor.

The persuasive qualities of metaphors

When former British prime minister Harold Macmillan talked about 'a wind of change sweeping across the continent of Africa' during a speech in South Africa in 1960, the image he planted in everyone's mind was of African nationalism as a force of nature.[2] This suggested an inevitability to the whole process: that there was little we could do about it. Now, I'm not suggesting Macmillan had spin doctors in Downing Street who advised him that this was the best metaphor, but rather that this was genuinely his view of the world, so he instinctively spoke through that metaphor. And the metaphor successfully persuaded: the British people came to share his sanguine view about the dismantlement of the British Empire. However, France's then president, Charles de Gaulle, had a different view of the world. He believed that African nationalism was very stoppable and so he used a different metaphor. The x=y that he used was African nationalists = vermin. This led people towards a different view: that insurgents should be eradicated.

By planting the idea of people as vermin, we legitimize execution. We see this in all sorts of scenarios. Mafia capos describe FBI informers as 'rats', the FBI responds in kind by talking about 'stamping out' criminals. Whenever we look at the language of genocides, vermin metaphors are never far from the scene. In Nazi Germany, the Jews were described as 'snakes'; in Rwanda, the Tutsi were characterized as 'cockroaches'; today, in the Western press, the metaphor of vermin is often used to talk about Islamic extremists: it is all about *'hunting'* them down, *'capturing'* them, *'trapping'* them, *'smoking them out'* from their *'lairs'*. The media described how Gaddafi was found in a pipe, Saddam Hussein was found in a hole and Bin Laden was always supposed to be hiding out in a cave, even though he was eventually found in a compound: all images that feed into the wider vermin metaphors.

These images are powerful and they have a persuasive effect: did it not strike you as a bit peculiar that in Britain – a country supposedly fiercely opposed to capital punishment – barely anyone so much as batted an eye-lid when Saddam Hussein was hanged on our watch? That is the power of metaphor.

Metaphors change behaviour

This is the thing: metaphors affect attitudes, values and behaviours. As already mentioned: a simple switch in metaphor can profoundly alter people's expectations about whether a share price is going to go up or down, thereby affecting whether they are likely to buy or sell.[3] Put simply, if the metaphor of a living being is used to talk about a share, people are more likely to think that share is going to go up. So, for instance, if you said that, earlier today, shares in Sainsbury's *'leapt'*, *'climbed'* or *'jumped'* – or, that they *'stumbled'*, *'fell'* or *'collapsed'* – then people would be more likely to believe that those shares would go up tomorrow than if an alternative metaphor were used.

Why? Well, you might have your own theory but I believe that we have a natural confidence in the ability of life forms to fulfil a given purpose. So our instinctive mind might envisage the share price 'getting back on its *feet*', '*climbing back* to its previous position' and even '*reaching up and touching* new heights'. You see how the metaphor predisposes and encourages us towards particular ways of thinking…

But let's scrub that idea. Let's try a different metaphor – a non-living metaphor. Let's try a machinery metaphor, so we might say that shares in GlaxoSmithKline 'were *propelled* higher', or '*driven* up' – or, perhaps, they '*plummeted*', or '*crashed*'. If we used this metaphor, people would be less likely to believe that shares would rise tomorrow. Why? Well, maybe, in our instinctive minds, we envisage that sooner or later they'll run out of *fuel*, need *repair* or require an *upgrade*.

That's the thing: metaphors can sometimes send completely the wrong image to that which is intended. I'll give you a personal example of this. Last year, my eldest daughter Lottie was diagnosed with Type 1 diabetes. She needs four insulin injections every day. At first, she hated needles and was terrified. We tried anything and everything to help her conquer her fear. One thing we noticed was how aggressive the language of diabetes was: the injections were called '*shots*' or '*jabs*', and '*lancets*' were used for blood tests. The metaphor was war. She was being encouraged to go to war with her own body. This image was even present in the comics she was given to 'help' her: soldiers were shown with machine guns loaded with insulin shooting down the nasty poisonous sugar molecules in her own blood-stream. No wonder she was terrified. We actively changed the language. We gave all her equipment names and said 'well done' to them when the injection was good and scolded them if they hurt Lottie. By personifying them, we made them into people: so she could learn to love them. And instead of giving her 'jabs', we gave her insulin. Today, she is completely relaxed about it. I don't pretend the language was the only thing that did the trick – she is so strong and incredibly brave.

Metaphors reveal our view of the world

The problem in the example of Lottie's insulin intake was that the NHS was using a metaphor that worked for them, not the patient. Clinicians always use war imagery: they talk about *fighting* cancer, *beating* illness, getting equipment to the *front line*. They like this imagery: it keeps them focused, it elevates their cortisol and adrenalin levels and it helps instil a strong sense of solidarity which permeates across the health service.

But this metaphor can negatively affect patients. Research showed that the use of war metaphors to cancer patients can cause feelings of self-loathing because they view themselves as the enemy. At the time of publication, a group of academics is compiling a metaphor manual to find those metaphors that positively influence the way patients feel.[4]

The NHS is an interesting case study for the use of metaphor. What you find is that different parts of the NHS use different metaphors that reflect their different outlooks, but then the use of these different metaphors reinforces organisational dividing lines. For instance, we all know there's a sharp divide between clinicians and managers in the NHS and you can see this in their language. Where the clinicians use war metaphors, managers seem locked within the metaphor of the NHS as a car. In recent years, they have launched a wellness *drive*, a dementia *drive* and an innovation *drive*. They have issued a *clinical dashboard*. They talk about putting patients in the *driving seat*. At one stage they issued an *'engagement tool kit'*. (I know... the mind boggles... What is an engagement tool kit? Presumably they meant 'a mouth').

People's metaphors reflect their outlooks. Different people have different outlooks. For me as a speechwriter this is a challenge. Because I write for third parties, I have to describe the world as my clients see it, not as I see it. So I analyse their metaphors: these can prove very revealing. It provides me with insight into their view of the world. I need to know whether they view their companies as people, organisms or machines. Their different outlooks determine whether they talk about the *'heart'* of the company, the *'nucleus'* of the company or the *'engine room'* of the company. Sometimes, even within the same company, different people have different outlooks and therefore speak through different metaphors.

I once analysed the language of a successful married couple who are in business together. The man sees business as a game, so he talks about *'rolling the dice'*, *'spinning the wheel'* or *'hitting the jackpot'*. His wife would never consider using such phrases. She sees running a business as a science: she talks about *'the essential elements'*, *'catalysts'* and *'explosive effects'*. In each case, they are instinctively revealing their own outlooks. She studied chemistry at Oxford, so this shapes her world-view; he, I imagine, might be found on a Saturday night at the local casino.

This is how metaphors can shed light onto character. My passion is music – my first job on leaving school was playing the piano in a restaurant (I know! I wish I'd never left...). I am still deputy keyboard player in a covers band: Soul Lotta Funk. You can find clues to my passion in my use of metaphor. I quite often speak through music metaphors: about being *'in harmony'*, or *'in concert'* and talk about *'grand crescendos'*.

Metaphors can even give clues to someone's political leanings. In the run-up to the 2010 general election in Britain, I led a research project on the metaphors of the different political parties, analysing hundreds of speeches by dozens of politicians, totalling more than a million words. It was gruelling, painful and totally exhausting work for the poor student lumbered with it (thank you, Scott Mason). But it was not in vain. Our work led to a valuable insight: there are critical differences in the metaphors of the main political parties.

The Labour Party uses conflict metaphors twice as often as the Tories – they talk about *'fighting* for our rights', *'defending* the NHS from Tory attack' and 'getting resources to the *front line'*. The Lib Dems favour journey metaphors: using them twice as often as the other parties, talking of *'moving forward'*, being at a *'fork in the road'*, taking *'a change in direction'* and so on. The Tories use nature and personification metaphors twice as often as the Labour Party: they talk about 'the *heart* of our communities', Britain 'standing *tall* in the world' and of Europe getting 'clogged *arteries'*.

You can see a connection between the metaphors that are used and the histories and philosophies of the three parties. After all, Labour was a party born in the revolutionary struggles of the 19th century so it's not too much of a leap to see why they might favour war metaphors. The Lib Dems see themselves as political progressives, so it's not surprising that they like journey metaphors. The Conservatives take a modest view about the role of the state, believing in laissez-faire economics and the way the world naturally sorts out problems on its own, so it is not so surprising that they might opt for nature metaphors.

Then, we had another light-bulb moment. We realised that the metaphors also linked with the parties' logos. The Tories' logo is the tree – nature. The Lib Dems' logo is the dove – journey. And Labour's logo may now be the red rose, but this dates back to a period when the strategy was to echo Tory language – Labour is still, however, at heart a revolutionary party that sings 'The Red Flag' at the end of each conference.

These metaphors become a common currency within the political parties. When everyone gets together, at branch meetings or party conferences, they use the same metaphor: this shows, instinctively, a shared perspective. They all see things the same way. They are safe. If different metaphors were used, it would be a sign of division. The leader's duty is to find metaphorical imagery that works for everyone. That is the Language of Leadership.

What is a good metaphor?

So what is a good metaphor?

In the Language of Leadership, if you want to win people over, listen to their metaphors. This gives you an insight into their world-view: an insight that can help you to win them over.

To win people over, listen to their metaphors

I'll give you an example. I quite often have to go out and sell my services: running workshops. If I'm meeting with an HR director, and they say to me that they want to *unlock* the communication potential in their board then I might explain to them that the '*key*' comes from the Language of Leadership workshops. This demonstrates that, at an instinctive level, I share their perspective. It shows they can feel safe with me. We are on the same side.

If, however, I replied, 'Well, the first thing we've got to do is shoot down this perception that communication doesn't matter', they might recoil slightly. They wouldn't like that. I'd have shown I saw the world differently. They would consider me part of a different tribe, a more aggressive tribe. Chances are that I wouldn't win the contract.

Mixed metaphors

In the 'key' example, I am using a metaphor that I know will resonate. I know it will work because I know this is the metaphorical image in the mind's eye of the person I am trying to persuade.

But many of the metaphors that are used in business and political communication have no persuasive effect at all. Many business metaphors are either muddled or misjudged. People might talk about mapping out a path of offensive actions designed to build advantage over the competition, which need to be well-executed and linked up throughout the whole business model, based on planting seeds from the foundations up. Your eyes might have already glazed over but I'm not making it up. This text is typical of writing that is endemic in business.

It sounds very authoritative and assertive but the problem is that there's no clear image for the instinctive brain to grasp. It reflects a confused perspective. The problem is mixed metaphors. We go from journey (mapping a path) to war (defensive) to construction (build) to spatial (over) to machine (linked) to design (model) to gardening (seeds) to building (foundations). It's metaphorical overload. At an instinctive level, such text repels because the language is so garbled, the vision so unclear. It would be simpler if they removed the metaphors entirely, or at least just came up with one simple one. A lot of the time, when you come up against some really garbled text, the best way to cut through it is by sorting out the metaphors.

Most of the time, I suspect the cause of such awful writing is 'drafting by committee': people with different perspectives get together to work on the same text. They disagree about the visions but no one wants to start an argument so they all stay quiet as long as their own metaphor makes it in.

More cynical readers might suspect that such text comes not from incompetence but design: that people deliberately use mixed metaphors to create text which is so garbled that it places it beyond scrutiny. The author is betting that no one will challenge the text because they fear that doing so might make them look stupid. They may well be right.

Below is an example of some text from McKinsey, the consultants. It is advice that they gave to the UK government, which sets out how savings of £20 billion could be achieved in the NHS. This is an extract from the executive summary:

> Achieving a step change in spend on health and healthcare services will require a compelling case for change; the use of formal mechanisms to drive through efficiency gains; deployment of WCC structures and processes; removal of national barriers to change; introduction of incentives schemes; and an increase in skills and capabilities to drive out costs.
>
> We recommend a nationally-enabled programme delivered through the SHAs and PCTs to drive through efficiency savings. The DH should take direct actions to capture some opportunities e.g. lowering tariffs. And should enable delivery by creating a compelling story, removing barriers, developing frameworks/tools and embedding the drive for efficiency gains within existing mechanisms e.g. WCC.[5]

What does this mean? If you asked 20 people, you'd get 20 different answers. It means everything and nothing. It is a shame that it was expressed in such a jumbled manner. With clarity of vision and expression, perhaps those savings could have been achieved. Suffice to say, savings of £20 billion have not been achieved in the NHS budget. On the contrary, spending keeps rising every year.

Misjudged metaphors

We have just looked at examples of muddled metaphors. Another common problem with metaphors is that they are misjudged: when someone uses a metaphor that means the right thing to them but which leaves the people they are addressing bristling.

Sporting metaphors are a good example of this. People who are into football might love talking about *goals*, leaving people on the *bench*, people being *offside*. It might work for them but, for many, it's a bit Alan Partridge. Others might talk about cricket – throwing someone a *googly*, taking a *wicket*, going out to *bat*. It doesn't work for everyone. In fact, when using any kind of sporting metaphors it's probably safe to assume you will alienate more people than you will entice.

War metaphors can also sometimes backfire. People might talk about fighting, weapons, troops and so on. To many, it feels too aggressive and swaggering. I've already talked about the proliferation of war metaphors within the British Labour Party. In the run-up to the 2015 general election, the then leader of the Labour Party, Ed Miliband, said he would fight to convince the public he had what it takes to be prime minister. Hmm. It strikes me that going to war with the electorate was probably not the best way to win them over. Reports emerged that he wanted to 'weaponise the NHS' during the general election. People were horrified at the suggestion that this much-loved institution could become a political weapon. The trouble was that, to Ed Miliband, politics was war and his metaphors reflected that. That may well have suited him as a way of thinking about politics, but if he wanted to win people over, he should have used a different mode of expression. Put simply, he should have spent less time speaking out of his arsenal.

Some use computer metaphors. These have become particularly fashionable in the last few years: not surprisingly, given the way that technologies are changing the way people think. More and more people are talking about 'resetting' companies or they talk about 'tapping into' various things; sometimes they talk about 'downloading' information from colleagues. This is a terribly depersonalising view of the world. 'We need to *reset* the Middle East', suggests an incredibly arrogant view. Millions of people can't be switched on and off like a computer. The metaphor comes from a desire to control, but it doesn't work if it's used on the people you want to control.

But perhaps the most prevalent problem metaphor is the car metaphor: the one I mentioned earlier that is so loved by NHS managers. This is the dominant metaphor in much organisational discourse. It's everywhere.

People talk about *'driving'* engagement, *'accelerating'* reform or *'changing gear'* on innovation. They talk about *'applying the brakes'*, *'parking'* ideas or even putting on *'turbo boosters'*. They talk about *'leveraging'* values, getting to the *'nuts and bolts'* and about certain things being *'pivotal'*. When things go wrong they *'run out of steam'* or *'break down'*: sometimes it might be because there was a *'spanner in the works'*.

The car metaphor works well for leaders when they are *thinking* about their organisations. It means they can make difficult operational decisions about things like redundancies in a detached, impersonal way, without considering the consequences for human lives and the emotional entanglement and pressure that brings. It also plays into their desire for control: it starts from the premise that their organisations are predictable, efficient, responsive and that all the answers lie at their fingertips. So, if they want to move forward all they have to do is turn the key, engage gears, put their foot on the gas and away they go. Isn't that image seductive? However, anyone with any real leadership experience will tell you that it doesn't really work like that. It is more like they get in the car, turn the key and think, hmm. What happened there? So, the car metaphor, whilst attractive for the leader, has no basis in truth.

But the worst indictment of machine metaphors is that they debilitate and depress the people they should inspire. Instead of making people feel safe, it makes them feel threatened. Because, if a company is a car and the leader is the driver, then what does that make the employees? It reduces them to parts and components – not there to innovate, not there to be creative, not there to think: purely there to fulfil a specific function; and if they do not fulfil these functions, then they will be removed and replaced without a thought. The machine metaphor strips staff of their own humanity. It introduces machine-like thinking. It brings people down.

Machine metaphors debilitate and depress

So where did this car metaphor come from? Why is it so endemic? My theory is that it emanates primarily from management consultants. The two founding fathers of modern management consultancy thinking – Frederick Winslow Taylor of Taylorism fame and Henry Gantt of Gantt chart fame – were both engineers and both writing at the turn of the 20th century, when the big thing in business was the mass production of the car: this would have made it a fashionable metaphor. At this time as well, large numbers of people did carry out work that was repetitive and unthinking, so the metaphor might have been appropriate. But the times have changed. Today, most organisations would claim to want people to be innovative, responsive and adaptive. If this is the case, we need a new set of metaphors. We need to move away from those metaphors that cast people as nuts and bolts in a big machine and find a new metaphor for new times.

Language of Leadership metaphors

Language of Leadership metaphors speak directly to the instinctive mind's two supreme needs: safety and reward. Metaphors like these will cross time, cultures and continents. They should achieve a universal resonance because they are speaking to universal needs.

So, in the rest of this chapter, I want to look more closely at five particular metaphors which fall within this category. Of course, I'm not suggesting these are the only metaphors that should be used and that they must be observed at all times; what I am suggesting is that these metaphors can lead you to new and exciting places. And, certainly, they will prove more successful than speaking about people as if they are components in a car.

Language of Leadership metaphors:

Personification;

Journeys;

Climate and nature;

Food and sustenance;

Families and friends.

Personification metaphors

When people don't like something, they naturally slip into machinery metaphors. They might say, 'I can hear the *cogs whirring*', if they are not impressed with someone's intellect, or they might say, if they are bored with their marriage, that things are *'ticking over'*. The flip side is that, when people feel affection for something, they naturally use the metaphor of personification. Keen gardeners say their plants look a bit *'thirsty'*. Keen boozers nip out for a *'cheeky pint'*. Proud homeowners talk about the kitchen as the *'heart of the house'*.

Look at the examples in Table 2.1 and you'll see what I mean.

If you've ever spoken to anyone involved with a big project, you'll have probably witnessed authentic personification metaphors. I know I do it. You can judge how pleased I am with my work by the metaphor I use. If I'm talking about a speech I think is going well, I might talk about the *heart* of the speech, the *spine* of the speech, or I might say it has got *legs*. If I am less happy, I might say it was *functional* or that I hadn't yet *assembled* all the pieces, slipping into that machine metaphor. That's the difference between the metaphor of personification and the dreaded machine metaphor: one communicates passion and one does not (Figure 2.1).

TABLE 2.1   **Examples of personification**

Charles Brower, advertising guru	'A new idea is delicate. It can be killed by a sneer or a yawn. It can be stabbed to death by a quip and worried to death by a frown on the right man's brow.'
Mary Portas, retailing guru	'High streets are the heart of towns and communities… Although some high streets are thriving, most have a fight on their hands. Many are sickly, others are on the critical list and some are now dead. We cannot and should not attempt to save every high street but my findings have led me to believe that unless urgent action is taken, the casualties will only continue to multiply.'
Jonathan Freedland, economics guru	'Confronted with the argument that the best way to breathe life into an economy gasping for air is not to strangle it tighter but to give it oxygen.'

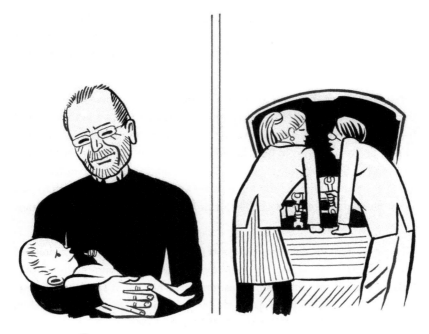

FIGURE 2.1 Personification or machine metaphor

Artists often personify. I recently saw a beautiful quote from Richard Curtis, writer of *Four Weddings and a Funeral* and other films. He said: 'The difference between having an idea for a movie and making a movie is the difference between checking out a woman on the other side of a room and being by her side whilst she gives birth to your third child.' That completely gets it: his movie is his baby. I feel the same about this book, incidentally. I'll be furious if the editor '*hacks out*' bits of text: I would consider that '*artistic murder*' (I bet I've just scared the life out of her…).

The great thing about personification is that it is wholly universal. It is a metaphor we can all understand, regardless of age, sex or religion. For all our differences, the one experience common to every person on the planet is inhabiting the human body. It is a truly global metaphor, stretching across languages, cultures and continents. In the West we often speak patronisingly about the Chinese notion of *'face'*, but the metaphor of face for human dignity is one that is equally prevalent in Western culture: in the UK, we talk about *'facing* up to problems' taking things at *'face value'* or receiving a *'slap in the face'*.

Personification is so powerful it crosses cultures, right down to the bits of the body we use. Sometimes, I work in Malaysia. The same metaphorical frames are often used in English and Malay. For instance, the eye is a metaphor for sexual interest in both languages. In the UK we talk about *'eyeing someone up'*, giving someone *'the eye'* or *'making eyes'* at someone; in Malaysia, they might call someone pervy a *'mata keranjang'*, which means *'a rough eye'*, and they describe flirting as *'bermain mata'*, which means *'playing eye'*.[6]

The nether regions also provide good metaphors. When I sent a draft of my first book – *Speechwriting: The Expert Guide* – to one of the world's leading experts on metaphor, I was terrified when I first saw his response. He had scrawled at the top of the chapter on metaphor: 'Shit'. Then I looked further down, '... that is a good metaphor too...'

He was right: shit is indeed a powerful and universal metaphor. Of course, the French talk of *'merde'* and in Britain many leaders talk *'shit'*, so to speak. It manifests in a myriad of forms. Boris Johnson talked about Ed Miliband 'emanating from the *bowels* of the trade union movement' (Ed Miliband = shit). Charles Saatchi says politicians are like *nappies* – they should be changed often (politicians = full of shit). Dennis Skinner said that Blair and Brown were two cheeks of the same *arse* (New Labour's policies = shit). Ronald Reagan said that government was like a *baby* – a huge appetite at one end and no sense of responsibility at the other (government output = shit).

Body metaphors are very powerful. When our metaphors refer to bodily actions – for example, 'this organisation has real *bite*' or we must *'grasp this opportunity'* – fMRI shows we activate the part of people's brains associated with these tasks. So they are actually visualising the act of biting or grasping. This is why personification is so effective: you literally get inside people's heads.

Personification in practice

A communications team might give a company *voice*. Our strategy team might be the *brains*. The surveillance team might provide *eyes* and *ears*. We might call ourselves a *listening* company or describe how we are *struggling* or *surviving*. We might talk about how we are 'standing *tall* in the world', '*seizing* opportunities' or '*reaching out* to our friends'. We need to understand what is our corporate *character*, what is our *identity* in the marketplace, what makes up our *DNA*. We need to know what are our *visions* and *values*. What is our *back story*? What are our chief *characteristics* and *attributes*? Why *do* people love us? Using this language feels very different to the language you get with machine metaphors, which suggests a very different view of the world. Table 2.2 takes a look at the two metaphors in comparison with each other.

Personification makes it personal. Entrepreneurs often talk about the companies they founded through the metaphor of personification. I once heard one entrepreneur talk about making cuts to his company after they had fallen on hard times. He said, 'We'd got *flabby*. That was the truth. We needed to lose *weight*. And there are lots of ways you can lose weight. You can go to Weight Watchers. You can go on the Atkins. You can get a gastric band inserted. Me, I went straight for amputation.' He got a big laugh. The metaphor was simple. The image was clear.

Personification can be deliberately contrived to cultivate intimacy: when Adam Smith talked about the 'invisible *hand* of the market', he planted in people's minds the ideas that markets were like people. This dealt head-on with the biggest criticism of Smith's economics: namely, that markets

TABLE 2.2 The patriot vs the social engineer

The Patriot	The Social Engineer
I'll tell you about British spirit…	Britain is firing on all pistons.
Responsibility is the life blood that runs through the veins and arteries of Britain.	We're wiring up different parts of society.
We can put Britain back on its feet so it stands tall in the world once again.	We are driving Britain back into pole position.

might be efficient, but they are uncaring; they can merrily put tens of thousands of people out of work without a thought. By using the metaphor of personification he opened up the possibility that the market might be capable of compassion. And Adam Smith knew what he was doing: he lectured on rhetoric at Glasgow University. His lectures are available on the web. They are very readable and they also leave you in no doubt that he knew the power of this particular metaphor.[7]

Most great brands are based on personification.[8] It helps people to love them. This is how we can see particular brands as friends. Just look around your kitchen: Mr Muscle, the jolly green giant, Uncle Ben. Look at some of the big ad slogans on billboards: 'Nothing hugs like Huggies' (Huggies Supreme diapers). 'The bank that likes to say yes' (TSB). 'Hotels with personality' (Best Western). Look around your house. My daughters never fail to get excited when Henry the vacuum cleaner rears his head. Establishing personality in objects, brands or companies brings them to life. Disney uses personification in animation. Great leaders use personification in persuasion. At the Mac launch, Steve Jobs talked about Macintosh as a person. He even had a conversation with her: 'Meet Macintosh.' With the iPhone he spoke of her as a beautiful woman, stroking her seductively and even going so far as to say, *'We made the button on the phone look so good you'll want to lick it.'* Hmm. Wonder what he had in mind there?

Great brands are based on personification

Some companies deliberately try to weave a human face into their design. When this works well, it activates the part of the brain that deals with facial recognition, causing what's known as physiognomic perception.[9] This is why watches in shops are always set at 10 to 2. Some houses are built to look like human faces.[10] VW camper vans and Mini Coopers are great examples: fMRI shows that when people see Mini Coopers, the part of the brain that deals with facial recognition lights up. It's one of the reasons why owners of these cars love them so much, giving them names and describing them as part of the family. I speak from personal experience here. I'm a VW owner. But I have a story here to illustrate the advantage that personification can give at the point of sale. When Lucy

TABLE 2.3 To metaphor or not to metaphor?

Metaphor of Personification	No Metaphor
Start your hols with Lolly the much-loved camper!! I bought this camper last year for me and my 4-year-old daughter but we are just so busy at the moment we have decided to sell her and get another van in the future when life is less hectic. Lolly is a great van. She always starts and passed her MOT in April this year first time without even any advisories!! (We were so proud of her.) She is not immaculate as you can see from the photos but she is fun. All the work to be done is cosmetic and not mechanical. It will be fun and not too expensive to get her back into shape and looking fabulous for the next adventure, festival or weekend away.	Volkswagen T25 Camper Van, 1981. 2-litre air cooled, recently restored. The restoration has included a roof-off professional re-spray, all rust removed and body panels replaced where required. New tyres with chrome hub caps and trims. A replacement engine has been fitted, which has been fully serviced with gaskets and seals. Carburettors serviced with gaskets and seals. Fuel tank has been replaced with a good second-hand tank that has been cleaned and painted. The engine starts and runs fine but would benefit from a rolling road fine-tune. The interior is clean and tidy.

and I were looking through eBay to buy our camper van, we came across the two ads shown in Table 2.3.

The one on the right is functional and informative: no more. It is not emotional and it is not persuasive. The one on the left does not simply personify, it also creates a colourful sense of character. We get a sense of Lolly as someone who is fun, easy-going and up for it: someone we might like to holiday with. In the end, the only one we went to see was Lolly, driving all the way to Worcester to see her and she was a total and utter rust bucket. Nevertheless, we had been motivated to see her, and that is the crucial first step in any sale. Speaking of first steps, let's move on to our next metaphor in the Language of Leadership: journey metaphors.

Journey metaphors

In his 2008 victory speech Barack Obama said to 250,000 people in Grant Park, Chicago: 'The road ahead will be long. Our climb will be steep. We may not get there in one year, or even one term, but America – I have never been more hopeful than I am tonight that we will get there. I promise you: we as a people will get there.'

This beautiful, much-quoted passage was redolent of so many great leaders of the past. All the great leaders use journey metaphors: from Jesus, Muhammad and Buddha to Mahatma Gandhi, Nelson Mandela and Martin Luther King. The journey metaphor is a powerful one in the Language of Leadership. When a leader describes a journey, they are speaking from a premise of leadership. I see the path ahead. That is one reason the journey metaphor has such power.

The other reason is because it activates the brain's reward system. If people can visualise where they're headed, they know when they're making progress, and their progress is rewarded with little squirts of dopamine along the way. This metaphor harks back to the journeys of our ancestors. It's also very popular in songs: 'Ain't No Mountain High Enough', 'Long and Winding Road', 'He Ain't Heavy'... to name just a few.

The journey can be as glorious and magnificent as we like. The more enticing and attractive the journey, the more there is for the reward system to get excited about. Let's move beyond just *moving forward* or being at a *fork in the road*. Take out your brightest paints and add some colour. Make it real. Make it vivid. Maybe the road we are travelling is bumpy? Maybe we should watch out for banana skins? Maybe there are bandits waiting around every corner prepared to steal our riches? Maybe the land we are walking upon is constantly shifting? Maybe we have got bogged down in mud? Maybe we're looking over a cliff edge? What about throwing in some nature metaphors: seeds being planted, flowers blooming or life flourishing – all of which are signifiers of a better journey ahead.

There's one other thing that should concern us about the journey ahead: the weather.

Weather

In the midst of Britain's 2010 general election, Gordon Brown said:

> Whilst we have come through the worst of this dreadful storm, the waters are still choppy. We have got through this storm together, but

there are still substantial risks ahead. It's about having the courage to set your mission and the courage to take tough decisions and stick to them without being blown off course. We are weathering the storm. Now is no time to turn back. We will hold to our course and we will complete this mission.

Are you seeing that? The storm metaphor is clear. It was also genius. The storm metaphor served two purposes. First, he was implying that the 2008 financial crisis was an act of nature. So it was not the fault of greedy bankers, timid politicians and ineffective regulators, instead it was an act of God. Indeed, isn't it curious that, despite multiple reports and inquiries showing failings at a regulatory, institutional and individual level, still no one has been sent to prison for their part in the financial crisis? The metaphor determines the response. Had a metaphor that pointed to man's involvement been used, such as a financial *crash*, or a financial *collapse*, then it may be that more people would have called for those responsible to be brought to justice. But no one challenged the metaphor: apart from, that is, my good friend Tom Clark who, in his fabulous book *Hard Times* (2014), rejected the *'storm'* metaphor. He said a storm would have resulted in rain falling equally upon everyone: this was more like a *typhoon*: devastating some communities, whilst leaving others untouched.

The other reason that Brown's metaphor was so powerful was because he positioned himself as captain of a ship sailing stormy waters. This was a great way to develop the journey metaphor. By conjuring up the image of a ship at sea, he strengthened his own position, making it less likely that people would try to remove him (as some senior cabinet ministers wanted). We can all understand that changing captains in the midst of a storm would have been madness. When one of his ministers, Hazel Blears, resigned in protest at Brown's premiership, she made her resignation speech wearing a brooch that sported the motif 'rocking the boat'. You see: once a metaphor is established, the image can prove irresistible, even to people with profoundly different perspectives.

Climate metaphors also often feature in the Language of Leadership and can be used by great leaders to strengthen their position. Tony Blair promised a new *dawn*. David Cameron talked about *sunshine* winning the day. Business leaders talk about *winds* of change, experiencing *gales*, being in the eye of a *hurricane*.

All of these metaphors hark back to our ancestral memory. They speak deeply to our instinctive mind's need for safety and reward. The enticing prospect of sunshine, that gentle glow in the distance, the warmth of sun on our skin. But likewise, talk of bitter chills, frosty outlooks or almighty storms can instinctively cause people to recoil. It's a safety instinct. One of the consequences of the 2008 financial crisis was lower levels of business start-ups and innovation. The storm metaphor would not have helped with this. After all, what do we do in storms? We hunker down, seek shelter, wait for the storm to pass.

Light and darkness metaphors can prove similarly effective: light is commonly regarded as a metaphor for good, whilst dark is a metaphor for bad. Movie directors always play with light to show us instinctively who are the good guys and who are the bad guys – great leaders can use the same technique, to create either push or pull. Where light leads to life, darkness delivers death, so these metaphors speak directly to the instinctive brain. The other metaphor that speaks straight to the instinctive is sustenance.

Sustenance metaphors

When we are on our journey, we need food to eat and water to drink. Without them, we know that we will surely perish. It is a matter of survival. The prospect of food and water gets our reward system going. They therefore make for powerful metaphors.

Information can be water – *trickling* down, *streaming* or *flowing*. This makes information sound appealing. Or we might found ourselves *drowning* in data or we might go on a *deep dive*. Less attractive.

But information can also be food. It harks back at least to the Bible and is currently particularly prevalent in IT. We all know *Apple*. Fewer people know that the Macintosh is actually a type of apple, common in

North America. Google uses the same food metaphor but they are not quite as health-conscious as Apple. They rename their Android operating system every year after a food that is naughty but nice – from *cupcake* to *doughnut* to *éclair*… Mmm. Then we get the Blackberry… This is a great metaphor. The metaphorical image of a Blackberry makes the literal reality of walking around with your office in your pocket appear not just attractive, but enticing. That is how metaphor can transform perception, but it is important that the image is just right. I was told that, when branding for the Blackberry was being discussed, for a time they were thinking of calling it a strawberry. But then they decided that a strawberry was a little too filling, too substantial. A blackberry seemed perfect. And it is, isn't it? A great example of the Language of Leadership. But I bet they go apoplectic every time they hear someone call it a 'crackberry'.

Money can also be water. The banks talk about *pools* of liquidity, cash *flow* and credit *droughts*. When times are tough, they might talk about turning off the *taps, freezing* assets and so on. The message here is that money is essential for our survival. It is a powerful idea. If capital systems stop flowing, we all die. But likewise money can also be food. We speak of *dough* and *bread*. If we felt a little short-changed we might talk about being fed crumbs from the table. Ideas can also be food. We speak of ideas being 'difficult to swallow', 'indigestible'; alternatively, they might be 'delicious' or 'tasty'. The prospect of a merger might be 'mouth-watering'. The metaphor of food always goes down a *treat*. It's easily *digestible*. It doesn't leave a bad *taste* in the mouth. Unless it is *pie* in the sky…

The idea of food invariably leads to the kitchen table, and around the kitchen table, who do we find but our friends and family.

Family and friends metaphors

We have a powerful instinct to be close to our friends and family: to belong. Talk of collaborative partners, stakeholder networks or business infrastructure does not arouse that instinct. What does work is images of friends and family, around the fire or the kitchen table: a sense of intimacy and affection.

The European Union is a *family* of nations. The union movement is a *brotherhood*. Sometimes, we can look at a nation as a *family*: in Britain, the government is the *father*, we have *mother* nature and the BBC is, of course, *Aunty* Beeb. Leaders can use this metaphor to entice people into the warmth of the family, but they can also flip it and turn it into a threat. In the referendum on Scottish independence, David Cameron warned that breaking up the United Kingdom would be like a 'painful *divorce*'. Now, I don't know about you, but I've never met anyone who has positive connotations with divorce. This was an effective metaphor which led the Scottish people away from independence.

But a different metaphor could have been used to create a completely different feeling. When Malaya was divided into Singapore and Malaysia in 1957, the then prime minister, Tun Abdul Razak Hussein, put it like this:

> Let us not regard the separation of Singapore from Malaysia as the two components of an unhappy marriage who, after being divorced, have recriminations and each fight for the maximum alimony or compensation for their own support, after the breaking of their life together. No, let us regard the separation of Singapore from Malaysia as similar to the separation of two Siamese twins: the separation of two children born together in the womb of Malaya. The operation of separating Siamese twins is delicate and intricate and is a great feat of modern science in this modern world. One has got to think of the nerve system, of the blood stream, of the bones and everything else by which they are joined. But modern science can now successfully separate two Siamese twins so that they can walk independently, act independently and prosper independently. And yet, throughout the world, you will find in every case of the separation of Siamese twins there remains a mental bond between them, even after their purely physical separation. They are still brother and sister.[11]

He rejected the divorce metaphor and used the metaphor of siblings who have to part for their own safety. This imagery still governs to this day the way that many Malaysians and Singaporeans feel about separation: they view each other with great affection, closeness and a strong sense of shared history. There is none of the bitterness and rancour that would arise from a messy divorce. Let's hope that if Scotland ever does break from the United Kingdom, this is the kind of imagery that we'd use.

Family metaphors are very effective for international relationships but they also work just as well within companies: working out who are your *friends*, your founding *fathers*, *sister* organisations and so on. Noticing the metaphorical names that are being used can provide insight into underlying problems.

I once worked with a major company that had just been through a demerger. I was instantly struck by how everyone in the company, across both sides, referred to it as a 'divorce'. This metaphor was clearly negative. We set out to create a new metaphor, a story of two companies who grew up in the same home, under the same roof, part of the same family, but who eventually grew so big, so strong and so successful that they needed to find their own space to grow even more. Subsequent staff surveys showed massive improvements. Instead of looking to the past, people started looking to the future. The demerger was seen as a positive opportunity for transformation.

Putting it into practice

There's a lot here. Don't be overwhelmed. Just an awareness of the way metaphors are used and their power gives you a huge advantage over your peers and your competitors, both in terms of understanding what other people are really saying to you and in finding ways to win them over.

An awareness of the effect of metaphors might also help you to avoid saying things that might inadvertently leave people feeling bad about themselves: as can happen not just with the car, computing or sporting metaphors I mentioned earlier, but even worse possible scenarios.

For example, one of my friends was recently going through a really hard time at work. He is a financial investigator and a critical piece of evidence had gone missing during an investigation. His manager said to him, 'Are you sure it's not festering on your desk?' He couldn't get this comment out of his mind. He woke up thinking about it in the early hours of Sunday morning. He cried to his wife. He couldn't work out why this had upset him so much. Yet it was really not surprising. His boss was talking about his desk as if it were a rubbish bin or a dirty wound. No wonder he was so offended.

So watch the metaphors you use, but also notice the metaphors used by others. Play people's metaphors back to them if you can: it will help you to win them over. If you take the minutes of a board meeting, you will notice the different metaphors that people use. This provides you with insights to their different outlooks. This helps you to speak in a way that fits in with their world-view. And when you notice people speaking in metaphors that conflict, you can help to mediate and find a new common metaphor that works for everyone.

If you want to take metaphor seriously, though, invest the time in getting your imagery right (Figure 2.2). You might consider running a workshop to help ensure that you and your top team literally have a shared vision. You might ask:

- What kind of person is our organisation? Are we intrepid, exciting explorers or serious, sober professionals? How do other people see us?
- Where are we going? What does our final destination look like? Can we tell it in full Technicolor™ glory? Are we headed to the Emerald City or are we just avoiding hell? What does the path ahead look like and what are the things we might encounter along the way?
- What will the climatic conditions be like? Is there wind in our sails or are we battling against a storm? How are we responding? Can we stay the course?
- What sustenance do we need? What do we need to keep fit, strong and healthy? Where do we find them? What will they taste like?
- Who are our friends along this journey? Who are our family? How close are our bonds and should we look to strengthen those bonds?

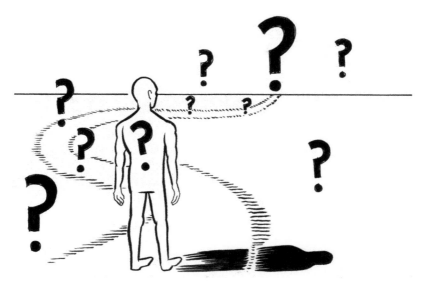

FIGURE 2.2 / **Know your metaphors**

Playing around with these questions – even getting an artist to help capture what you are saying visually – could help you to create a whole new language and vocabulary that will speak to people's most overwhelming instinctive needs. Of course, these are not the only metaphors you should use. There are endless possibilities. What matters is that your image works.

Imagery is crucial in leadership. The image of the leader is particularly important. And that is what we explore in the next chapter, 'The Look of Leadership'.

chapter 3

The Look of Leadership

'Only the convinced convince.'

Max Dessoir, French psychologist

A FTSE CEO once invited me along when he was going 'walkabout' around his company. This was a great opportunity for me as his speechwriter. Going walkabout is one of the biggest tests of any leader. This is when you learn what they're really like. A whole day cannot be acted: sooner or later the mask must slip, producing one of those 'moments of truth' when a person's real identity is revealed. One of my best friends has met his CEO three times. Each time, they have exactly the same conversation. 'What's your name?' 'And what do you do?' 'That sounds very important. Keep it up.' His boss fails that 'moment of truth'.

Well, with my client, there was no such moment. The whole day, he was on fire. When he went into a room, it was as if 20 people walked in. In conversation, he radiated such warmth, even when the topics being discussed were not the most scintillating. When we got into the car at the end of the day, I asked, 'How did you manage to look so interested all day?' He looked taken aback. 'I am interested!' he said. I felt ashamed to have doubted him.

This chapter is about the look of leadership. This is not to say that there is a single look of a leader. But we do know that the instinctive mind is attracted to specific types of people: those who offer the promise of safety and rewards. So this chapter looks at how leaders can do that.

There are all sorts of things we could talk about. I've focused on three key attributes. Great leaders must appear strong, sincere and *sexy*.

Great leaders must appear strong, sincere and sexy

/ Strong

The greatest leaders in history have all seemed strong: though all in different ways. Some built strong into their names: William the Conqueror, Richard the Lionheart, Alexander the Great. Others built strong into their expressions: Malcolm X's clenched fist, George W. Bush's swagger, John F. Kennedy's wagging finger. Others talked strong: 'We shall fight them on the beaches', and 'It is a cause for which I am prepared to die'. The rest actually were strong: Arnold Schwarzenegger with his extraordinary fitness regime, Nelson Mandela working out in prison; and the more recent crop of athletic-looking leaders: the Obamas in the gym, Christine Lagarde's daily swimming and Tim Cook with his 5am workouts.

Strength is not necessarily physical fitness – Winston Churchill, John Harvey Jones and Henry VIII were hardly pictures of health – but nevertheless they were like bulldogs. You wouldn't mess with them. That is what meets our instinctive needs. People need to know that their leader will defend them from external threats. They must look as if they will fight tooth and nail on our behalf. It's not about whether they *are* strong, it's whether they *seem* strong. Appearance is what matters, not reality. It might seem superficial, but this is the way leaders are judged. Famously in the 1960 Nixon–Kennedy presidential debates, those who listened on the radio thought that Nixon was the winner, those who watched it on TV thought Kennedy came out best. The difference was appearance: where JFK looked tanned, slim and healthy, Nixon spilled out over his ill-fitting suit, twitched and sweated. JFK looked the stronger: he won.

Women leaders do not have a get-out clause: great women leaders also appear strong. Think Boadicea, Britannia, Joan of Arc and Cleopatra.

Remember the archetypal image of Margaret Thatcher – atop a tank, wearing a wraparound headscarf, looking not dissimilar to the Boadicea statue that stands by Westminster Bridge.

Thatcher developed an image of enormous physical strength even though, in truth, she would probably have lost an arm-wrestle with any one of the so-called 'wets' in her Cabinet. It's not *being* strong that matters in the Language of Leadership, it's *seeming* strong. The Look of Leadership is largely an illusion. And Thatcher certainly seemed strong, even though it was all a creation: her breathy, low voice, her broad shoulder pads and high heels and, of course, the metaphoric imagery of the 'Iron Lady' (a phrase that was actually coined by the Russians).

The Look of Leadership is largely an illusion

When Hillary Clinton stood for the Democratic nomination for president in 2008, she took advice from Mark J. Penn, a top US communications guru. Some of his advice leaked. In one particularly controversial section, he advised Clinton that the American people regarded the president of the US as the 'father' of the nation. He argued that they were not prepared to regard the president of the US as 'mother' of the nation; but, they were prepared to see a woman play the role of 'father' of the nation. Penn pointed out that, in Western politics, there was only one real precedent of a woman playing the role of 'father' of the nation, and that was Margaret Thatcher.

So Thatcher borrowed from Boadicea and Hillary Clinton borrowed from Thatcher. This is what happens in the Language of Leadership. Great iconic images are passed down through generations like old clothes, bestowing timeless and magical powers upon those who wear them. There is no shortage of strong iconic images to draw from. Many British leaders go all Churchillian when the occasion requires – indeed, if Boris Johnson's political career ever stalls, he could make a fair fist of life as a professional Churchill impersonator. Likewise, many American leaders often go all JFK. We all know the signs: we know what they're doing, they know what they're doing, and everyone's happy. It's a shortcut to saying 'this is who

I am'. Barack Obama sometimes strikes me as a combination of Lincoln, Kennedy and Martin Luther King.

The voice also indicates strength. I've already mentioned how Thatcher lowered her voice. A low voice is a sign of strength. In all eight presidential elections between 1960 and 2000, the candidate with the lower voice won the popular vote.[1]

Pause to show strength. In ordinary conversation most people speak over 200 words a minute. Great speakers tend to clock in at around 90 words a minute. They achieve this rate not by speaking in a slow, tedious, patronising way, which would rapidly become very irritating and annoying, but by leaving pauses between each idea: pauses that give people time to think. These pauses would feel unnatural in a normal conversation – indeed any pause of more than a second can feel like an 'awkward silence' – but, from a leader, they signify strength.

One of the other things that makes leaders look strong is their willingness to stand alone. You think of the imagery of the modern TED talk: the leader alone, on the stage, not hidden behind the lectern, but out there, vulnerable, saying 'this is me, take me as I am'. That image alone is an expression of strength.

Great leaders *do* stand alone. That solitude speaks to our instinctive understanding of the leader's role within a group. If you've ever been to the zoo, and seen the head honcho gorilla or lion or chimpanzee, you'll know what I mean, they are sitting slightly apart, slightly different to everyone else, but there is no question that they are the one who wields all the power.

Leaders *are* different to everyone else. This feels counter-intuitive. There is a widespread perception that leaders emerge from the mainstream or the establishment. This is wrong. Real leaders operate outside of the mainstream. By definition, a leader must sit slightly outside of the rest: otherwise they are not leading, they are simply standing in line.

Just think of great leaders from history. Winston Churchill and Margaret Thatcher were both outsiders in the Tory Party: Churchill crossed the floor twice in his career. Tony Blair was an outsider in the Labour Party.

And Barack Obama was a definite outsider as he rose up within the Democratic Party. Mandela was an outsider in the ANC: the organisation that gave him his first platform considered him a nightmare, as he describes in his memoirs. Gandhi was also an outsider: preaching peace when many of his contemporaries advocated revolution.

You get the same phenomenon in business. Steve Jobs, Richard Branson and Rupert Murdoch played on the fact that they were outsiders throughout their careers. Even as they became the establishment – becoming super-rich and market dominant – they still constantly adjusted their image so that, in perception terms at least, they remained the rebels, not the insiders. It's no coincidence perhaps that all of them have brushed up against the law at some point. These people are separate from the rest.

It's the outsiders we are drawn to instinctively. That is why, if you ever watch a panel programme, such as the BBC's *Question Time*, it is always the odd one out who gets the loudest cheers: the Russell Brand, Salman Rushdie or Nigel Farage character. When John Lydon appeared on *Question Time* recently, he received seven times as much applause as the next most popular panellist, never mind the bollocks he was actually saying.

The outsider must clearly be strong, but they must also be credible.

Sincere

People are very good at sniffing out liars. Our instinctive minds do all of the hard work, scanning for signs of insincerity, then sending up a vague sense of unease. We just know when someone's not quite right. The instinctive mind forms this judgement by scanning for signs of inconsistency: inconsistency between what people are saying and what their body reveals. For instance, if someone comes up to you and says 'Great to see you!' with open arms, a beaming smile and then clutches your hand and shakes it vigorously, you would assume that was okay. If, however, someone said, 'Great to see you', but their feet were pointing away from you, that might set warning lights flashing: the direction in which someone's feet are pointing always gives away where they want to be. The point is that the body language must match the verbal: if they are not matching, it is the body language that will prevail.

There was research carried out in the 1970s by a guy called Professor Mehrabian. He examined how people respond when there is a conflict between what someone is saying and how they are saying it. He assessed the relative importance of people's words (their verbal com- munication), their tone of voice (their vocal communication) and their body language (their physical communication). He concluded that, where there is a conflict, the verbal content (i.e. words) only accounts for 7% of the communication. The rest is body language and tone of voice. That's a whopping difference: it means that what we say is far less important than how we say it.

Words only account for 7% of communication. The rest is body language and tone of voice

It sounds far-fetched and some people have challenged Mehrabian's con- clusion, but just think about your personal experience. I know very well that if I sense Lucy is a bit out of sorts and I ask her what's up and she says 'Nothing' through gritted teeth, then I know I've done something wrong… (In fact, when she reads this section, I guarantee she will purse her lips slightly. I will ask her what's wrong; she'll reply, 'Nothing'.)

This is the thing: as leaders, you must be aware that your bodies give you away. As Freud said, 'He that has eyes to see and ears to hear may convince himself that no mortal can keep a secret. If his lips are silent, he chatters with his fingertips; betrayal oozes out of him at every pore.'[2] Or, as Roald Dahl put it: 'If a person has ugly thoughts, it begins to show on their face. If you have good thoughts, it will shine out of your face like sunbeams and you will always look lovely.'[3] The truth outs. You cannot stop your instinctive brain communicating your real feelings: that is what happens. So, bear it in mind: if you respect people, people will see that respect; just as, if you do not respect people, that will also be clear.

Such inconsistencies are not always visible to the naked eye but they will not escape the attention of the instinctive brain. Even when we are trying desperately hard to mask our feelings, we give away micro-expressions, instantaneous flashes, where our true feelings manifest, just for the tiniest fraction of a second. So, for instance, if I am making a speech to 500 people at Chelsea Football Club, I might say, 'I'm delighted to be here…' but, if you filmed my speech and played it back slowly, then you would probably see one-hundredth of a second's worth of apprehension. We simply can't keep our true feelings trapped: they escape.

Police investigators are wise to this: indeed, the phrase 'micro-expressions' was first used by an FBI investigator called Paul Eckman. If law enforcement officers are interrogating a murder suspect about what he did with a knife, his verbal response might be 'I never touched it!' but his physical response might betray him: he might make a motion with his right hand showing he cast the knife to one side.

So the best advice to leaders is to be honest. There is a tension here, however. Honesty is not always the best policy. If you look back at the pantheon of great leaders in history, you would find that what binds them together is not honesty. If you ask me what I think is the most honest business speech of the last 30 years I would have to say Gerald Ratner's speech to the Institute of Directors at London's Albert Hall in 1991 when he said, 'People ask me, "How can you sell cut-glass sherry decanters complete with six glasses on a silver-plated tray… all for £4.95?" I say, "because it's total crap".' That was a completely honest answer – and what happened? Within 24 hours he was front-page news in the red tops, within a week the company's share price had lost half a billion and within months he had been forced out of the company that bore his own name. There have been similar more recent examples, such as when Tony Hayward, the CEO of BP, said after the Deepwater Horizon oil spill crisis in 2010, 'I just want to get my life back.' Or when Matthew Barrett, the CEO of Barclays, said to a House of Commons select committee that he would never borrow on a credit card.

Instead of all-out honesty, the trick is to create the illusion of honesty. It is about sending little signs to suggest you are being totally honest whilst actually being quite careful and controlled about what you conceal and reveal.

Boris Johnson does this beautifully. I've seen him at the back of conference halls, just before being introduced, deliberately ruffling his hair and pulling his shirt out from his trousers. It makes him appear honest, more sincere. Boris Johnson is actually very guarded and point-blank refuses to discuss whole chunks of his life.

One way that leaders create this illusion of honesty is when they say: 'My PR people will probably kill me for saying this but…' and then they say something about not knowing how to turn on a computer or being a huge *Star Trek* geek. This is great. People love it. They feel that they are getting the real person. I'll let you into a secret as well: it's not just the public who love it; their PR people love it too.

Sometimes, honesty can be hard to achieve because the leader actually doesn't believe what they are saying. This happens more frequently in public life than we might care to admit. It is the nature of collective responsibility that any leaders who speak on behalf of any group or organisation will, on occasion, have to make arguments that they do not wholly believe. I know cabinet ministers who argued against the Iraq War in private whilst defending it in public. I've seen businesspeople riddled with doubts about a particular announcement, but who went out and sold it like it was the best thing since sliced bread. I've seen leaders who are cynical and sceptical backstage turn into devout evangelists once the cameras start rolling. How do they do it?

To hark back to the Max Dessoir quotation at the beginning of this chapter: to convince we must be convinced. Tony Blair's wife, Cherie, once said of him, 'Once Tony believes something, he believes it 110%.' It's true. Look at any of his performances. He is never half-hearted. He always seems to speak from the absolute pit of his being. Go to YouTube and watch his People's Princess speech – he looks completely distraught, whilst performing a note-perfect rendition of his speech. Look at his 'forces of conservatism' speech – when he left the conference platform, shirt dripping with sweat. Look at his Iraq speeches in the House of Commons, where he sounded genuinely terrified at the prospect of an assault on London.

That was part of the secret of his success: he could appear to speak with utter conviction on any issue from the sublime to the mundane. He appeared convinced, and that made him convincing. This made him seem simultaneously sincere and strong. As one politician said to me at the time of the Iraq crisis: the British people will forgive a leader who is wrong, but they will never forgive a leader who is weak or indecisive.

I always believed that Gordon Brown's problem was that he rarely seemed to speak with great conviction. He seemed to be a man in perpetual conflict: a conflict between what he felt to be morally the right thing to do, and what he thought was the right tactical position. This manifested in a gap between what he said and how he looked. So Brown would say he was listening and learning but thump his fist on the lectern at the same time. It was not very convincing.

The whole excruciating Mrs Duffy episode demonstrated for me the tension at the heart of Gordon Brown's public image. To me, he sounded wholly sincere when he was recorded calling Mrs Duffy a 'bigoted woman', when he believed he was speaking privately to an aide. When he later apologised to Mrs Duffy, in what must go down as one of the most demeaning moments in prime ministerial history, a false grin wedged his face – and I did not think we were seeing the sincere Gordon Brown. I don't think anyone else did either. I actually think that was a critical error of judgement on his part – he would have done better to stand by his original sentiment, whilst apologising only for Mrs Duffy's hurt feelings – but that's another story.

Bill Clinton was another leader who could seemingly summon up conviction in a flash. When he looked the nation in the eye and said, 'I did not have sexual relations with that woman', his face betrayed no signs of insincerity. Experts in body language have pored through the video tapes and said he betrayed none of the typical signs of deception. The only way that he could have been so convincing is if he had actually convinced himself. Who knows what mental contortions he went through – but it worked: he convinced himself and therefore he could convince others. Maybe he figured it was not he who had sexual relations with Miss Lewinsky, but the cigar?

Sexy

Despite Clinton's misdemeanours, he remains a powerful global leader. Likewise, in the UK, when the press revealed that Paddy Ashdown (or 'Paddy Pantsdown' as he then became known) had been having a fling with his secretary behind his wife's back, his ratings went up. This takes us to the third element of the look of leadership: we also demand that our leaders are just a little bit sexy. There is a good reason why our instinctive brains might draw us towards leaders like that: we must ensure continuance of the tribe, so virility and fertility are crucial traits in a leader. It is telling that all three of the current crop of party leaders in the UK at the time of writing this book – Ed Miliband, David Cameron and Nick Clegg – had very young children. This satisfies the instinctive brain's desire to know that these are leaders who can continue the tribe.

We don't much like leaders who are unattractive. There aren't many leaders with greasy hair, bad skin or poor personal hygiene. They need to be relatively easy on the eye. Jonathan Charteris-Black, in his book *The Communication of Leadership*, said that one of the reasons why Labour fared so badly under Michael Foot and Neil Kinnock was because they 'did not have appearances which were conducive to an age of media representation'.[4] I think this is a polite way of saying they were too ugly.

There is a tension here. Sexy = good. Pervy = not so good. I once saw someone speaking to staff who, mid-presentation, clicked to YouTube to show a video. Now YouTube, as most of you will know, has this helpful 'videos recommended for you' function based on previous searches. The video that YouTube suggested for our illustrious leader was 'young secretary bends over in tight leather skirt'. There was a gentle thud as 250 jaws simultaneously hit the floor.

The Look of Leadership in practice

If you're looking for practical guidance on how to look strong or sexy, you're reading the wrong book. Those looking for advice on that kind of stuff should go out and buy a copy of *GQ* or *Vogue* or get a personal trainer: they'll put you on the right track.

But I will say that I know there are certain things that won't do you any harm. Buy some clothes that make you feel great. Not only will the new clothes help you to look the part, status symbols such as new clothes raise our serotonin levels – and high serotonin levels are associated with leadership. So, there you go. A scientific justification to go shopping!

I'd also suggest getting some kind of physical activity in your life as a habit. I'm struck by how many of my clients do regular exercise – from kayaking to cycling to Formula 3 racing. It can't hurt. We know endorphins make us feel powerful and that can't be bad. You need to prove you can look after yourself. If you can look after yourself, you are worthy of looking after the tribe. If you can't look after yourself, your leadership credentials must come into question. You can't afford to be ill.

I remember once listening in to a C-suite call between a CEO and his top team. Half-way through the call, the CEO had a coughing fit that lasted a good 10 to 15 seconds. It was excruciating: there were 400 people waiting on the end of the line. The call was two hours long but all anyone remembered was the coughing fit. These things are worrying in leaders: leaders must appear good to last.

As far as sincerity goes, I can offer some more advice: the easiest way to look credible is to be credible. Only say things you can really believe. Don't kid yourself into believing you're a great liar. Chances are you're not. The truth will out. You will be sussed out. So if you are required to say something you don't entirely believe, then spend as little time on that as possible before moving on to something you can say with sincerity.

Don't kid yourself into believing you're a great liar. Chances are you're not

Let me give you an example. Say there is someone in your team who you really don't like. Now, imagine they come up to your desk one day, sigh and say, 'I've got some bad news. I'm leaving. I've got another job.' Of course, your instinctive mind will be elated but you know you can't show that. You know you should say something like, 'Oh, what terrible news: we're really going to miss you.' But as you say it, your face contorts with the pressure of delivering such a blatant lie. It's your dastardly instinctive brain that is bursting to reveal your true feelings of elation. The person you're talking to knows you're lying. You know you're lying. It's all a bit awkward.

So how can you avoid this? Try saying something closer to the true emotion you have in your heart. That will allow you to release your smile legitimately. So how about, 'That's great news. How fantastic for you. Sometimes you've got to take a leap in life. Now tell me more about this job. Are you excited?' You haven't lied and you've released your authentic emotion, which was joy.

Appearances are everything for the leader. One of the other things the leader must appear is purposeful. And purpose is the next secret we unravel from the Language of Leadership.

4

Inner Purpose

'No wise fish would ever go anywhere without a porpoise.'
Alice in Wonderland, Lewis Carroll

Whenever I go to a conference or event, I am always struck by how some people just stand out: they have a kind of magical buzz around them, an aura that energises all around. When they speak, everyone listens. When they move, others follow. You know the kind of people I'm talking about: the kind you just know are standing behind you, even without having to turn around. These people are natural leaders; their every word and action speaks leadership in volumes. They stand in marked contrast to the ordinary Joes and Josephines cowering away in the corners, clutching their tea and biscuits. The leaders know why they are there and they know what they are doing. They have purpose. Purpose is critical to the Language of Leadership.

The instinctive brain is naturally drawn to people with purpose. Purposefulness is an incredibly attractive trait. I bet you can remember occasions when friends or colleagues of yours have embarked on big missions – running marathons, starting businesses, climbing mountains, building houses or some such endeavour. Whilst they were pursuing their goal, weren't they giving off a buzz?

There is a good reason why we are attracted to purposeful people: it is they who are most likely to keep the tribe safe. They are the ones who will deliver progress and change. They are the ones who will take us forward. So our instinctive brain gets us behind them. It does so in three ways. First, purposeful people activate our mirror neurons. Second, they instil in us a sense of purpose which activates our reward system, getting the dopamine flowing. Third, we feel a sense of connection with them, getting the oxytocin flowing.

Purposeful people activate our mirror neurons

We end up mimicking them. If you want to see how this happens, search on YouTube for 'Guy starts dance party at Sasquatch music festival'. You see a guy dancing with utter purpose, whilst everyone else walks around in a bit of a daze (as you do, at festivals). First, a few people gather around and copy him. Then, before long, there are dozens. Then, there are hundreds. Before he knows what's going on, the whole festival is copying his vaguely insane dance moves. It's an inspiring video, whether you like dancing or not. It has had 12 million views on YouTube (http://www.youtube.com/watch?v=GA8z7f7a2Pk).

This is the power of purpose. Purposeful people make things happen. When there are no purposeful people around, nothing happens. It is leaders who step in and fill that void. So, ask yourself: what's your purpose?

Great leaders have crusades/missions

Great leaders have a higher purpose. This purpose energises them and those around them. It means they speak with utter conviction, like a force of nature. Think of Mandela, Gandhi, Branson, Jobs, Lennon, Geldof. These were people on crusades, crusades that came from somewhere deep within – what in Asian culture they call their *hara* or *chi*. In English, we might say they were led by their gut, or that they had a calling. In fact, research has shown that a disproportionate number of leaders do describe their work as a 'calling'.[1] It's more than just a job.

There is a connection between religion and leadership. I've often noticed that there is a disproportionate share of leaders at the top of both business and political life who are not just believers but active churchgoers. Many are preachers. I've often wondered why. Maybe their spirituality gives them a wider sense of purpose? Maybe their religion gives them a greater faith and optimism in the intrinsic value of other people, which helps them to win people over? Maybe there is a genetic capacity to believe, and that helps them to evangelise: if they can have a huge faith in God then maybe it's not too much of a leap to also have great confidence in a strategic plan.

Certainly, there are strong religious undercurrents in the Language of Leadership: great leaders often speak in terms of their 'mission', 'devotion', 'evangelising', 'preaching' and 'converts'. They are enthusiasts (in fact, the etymology of this word also actually has religious origins: deriving from the Greek – *'en theo'* – meaning 'god inside'). This language rubs off on those around them. This is how a mission is created. It's how a movement is born.

But how do you find this big purpose? Most of the time it's a simple matter of presentation. It's the way you look at it.

Get a vision

There's an old story. You walk past a building site. Three builders are there, laying a wall. You ask them what they're doing. The first one says he's laying bricks. The second one says he's building a wall. The third one says he's building a cathedral that will provide a beautiful place for people to worship for hundreds of years to come. Who do you think works the hardest? Who do you think enjoys their work the most? Which of them do you think goes home happiest at the end of the day?

The story is old but it makes an important point: that it's your responsibility as a leader to make people feel good about what they do: not as an act of benevolence or charity, but because that's how you get the best out of people. When people believe they are contributing to a higher purpose, they will give you their heart and soul. That is a massive prize. It's what leadership is all about.

But what is that higher purpose? It is not always immediately apparent in politics or business. After all, the statutory defined purpose of any corporation is 'to maximise returns for shareholders'.[2] Likewise, the governing purpose of most political parties, if we're really honest, is about winning and holding power. These purposes fail because they are not emotive. Great leaders pursue missions that are deep and meaningful.

Great leaders pursue missions that are deep and meaningful

There is a famous story: when the man on the moon mission was under way in the 1960s, John F. Kennedy went to visit NASA to see how work was progressing. Whilst he was there, he saw a man wearing a white coat and cap. Kennedy stopped and asked the man what he did. The man replied, 'I'm helping to put a man on the moon.' Mr Kennedy smiled. 'Yes, but what's your job?' 'Oh,' said the man, 'I'm a janitor in block D8. I'm just off to start my shift.'

Putting a man on the moon is an example of a truly great and inspiring vision: one that will inspire people the length and breadth of any organisation, having as much resonance with the leaders at the top as it will with the cleaners and janitors at the bottom. It works because it's big, but it also works because it's vivid. It provides a clear image, which will lodge in the instinctive mind. Not every organisation can have as its mission 'to put a man on the moon', but every organisation can and should find a higher calling. It's about finding an emotional long-term strategy that links with the day-to-day short-term tasks. It's about connecting the mundane with the sublime.

If you want to see this kind of thing in practice, take a look around companies such as GlaxoSmithKline or Unilever. Employees at both of those companies are filled with mission. Glaxo is saving lives – make no mistake. When the Ebola crisis struck and the whole world was grappling for a cure, that whole company was enveloped with purpose.

Energy flowed from top to bottom, people working longer and later to find that cure.

Unilever is also a company filled with a sense of purpose. Did you know that every single day 5000 children under the age of five die because of disease and poor hygiene? Unilever employees know this number well because it is their mission to halve it. If they could just get more kids in developing countries to wash their hands with soap, they could save millions of lives. What would you rather do with your time? Save lives or sell soap?

This is how companies find their callings and it is how great leaders get people giving their all. There's heaps of research to show that people work harder when they believe their work is in pursuit of a noble cause.[3] The world has moved on from the old model of 'corporate social responsibility' that existed in the 1980s, where companies could act as unethically as they liked as long as they threw a few quid at local projects every now and then. These days, business is all about how you align commercial aims with a moral imperative and use that to achieve great results: for the business and for the world.

Great leaders get this and always have. Henry Ford's mission was 'democratising the automobile' – putting a car within reach of every working man and woman on the planet. Bob Shapiro's first speech as Monsanto's CEO made a rallying cry to eradicate global hunger. Laura Bates, the founder of the Everyday Sexism Project, sees it as her mission to spread genuine equality around the world. These are great, noble, inspiring aims: just what we want in the Language of Leadership.

The trick is to find the biggest emotional goal that relates to your strategic goal. Don't hold back: the bigger the better. Jim Collins says that leadership goals should be 'big, hairy and audacious'.[4] The Beatles never said they wanted to be the biggest band in Liverpool. They set out to be the 'toppermost of the poppermost'.

Finding a noble mission which wraps around an organisation can have the most amazing effect. So find your purpose. Find the link with your organisation. Then make sure everyone knows about it.

Visual progress

It's not enough to just announce a big vision. People must see progress against their vision.

People must see progress against their vision

Think back to our alter ego on the mountain. We were motivated by a vision of a blackberry bush. As we got closer to that bush, the vision became clearer, so increasing quantities of dopamine were released to motivate us onward. The instinctive brain has this clever reward system built in to ensure we don't collapse to the ground with tiredness in the middle of a journey, but keep going in pursuit of the grand prize. But it is all based upon visual signs of progress.

For leaders, this means that visions must be described clearly, but progress must also be clearly demonstrated against that vision. That is how we keep people motivated. There is one major retail company I know that begins every internal meeting with a customer talking about how they have personally benefited from the company's services. This keeps everyone's eyes firmly focused on the human benefits. It is very motivating. Everyone gets a bit buzzy at these meetings. That's the dopamine.

The Open University's charismatic vice chancellor, Martin Bean, often talks publicly about how it is his ambition to put a great education within reach of everyone on the planet. He whips up huge enthusiasm. You can see the joy in people's eyes as he tells individual stories about people's lives enriched and improved by the OU.

In both cases, people can see progress against the vision. We all need that to keep going. It is the satisfaction of crossing something off a 'to do' list. My ever-increasing word count whilst writing this book has kept me going. A good leader will create visual progress points to keep people highly motivated.

One of the most motivating environments I have ever worked in was as a teenager doing telesales. I worked with 20 other youngsters in a packed room above a sex shop in London's King's Cross, cold-calling customers from the *Yellow Pages*. Every sale achieved was written up on a huge whiteboard. It was a clear visual record of progress. We knew how well we were doing, how much money we were making (it was all commission-based) and how far off our target we were. Our target was one sale a day – which meant 300 rejections a day – but we didn't notice the rejections: when the sale was written up we felt *amazing*. Dopamine. Serotonin. Sheer joy.

Whatever the vision, people must see progress (Figure 4.1). If the vision seems too distant, people start to drift away. I've seen too many grand ideas that have fizzled into nothing over the years… In 2000, the European Union announced at the Lisbon Summit that it would match US productivity levels within ten years… It was an exciting vision at first but a lack of progress was apparent within a couple of years. At that point, supporters walked away. The brain's reward system is not only good at recognising progress, it is also good at recognising a lack of progress – and it marks that with the opposite of a dopamine high: it makes people feel rubbish.

FIGURE 4.1 / **Rewards and purpose**

People also need to feel involved: they must see a genuine link between their day-to-day work and the grand vision. If they lose that link, there is also a risk they will walk away. I know a lot of people who have become involved at a local level in politics but who left because they could not see any connection between what they were doing and the party's success nationally. They became disillusioned and disengaged.

Leadership is about giving people a sense of involvement and fulfilment. It's about making dreams come true. That's what leaders do. For the rest of us mere mortals, our dreams don't go beyond the kitchen table after a couple of bottles of Beaujolais. Leaders are different: that's why we follow them.

In the early 1980s, Steve Jobs famously lured top PepsiCo executive John Scully to come and join Apple with the immortal line, 'So. Do you want to carry on selling sugary water for the rest of your life or do you want to come with me and change the world?' What do you think Scully did? You're dead right. Scully and Jobs worked successfully together at Apple until it became apparent that, although they shared a vision, they could not see eye to eye on how to achieve that vision. This takes us to the next chapter in the Language of Leadership: empathy.

5

 chapter

Empathy and the Power of Nice

'Too often we underestimate the power of a touch, a smile, a kind word, a listening ear, an honest compliment, or the smallest act of caring, all of which have the potential to turn a life around.'

Leo Buscaglia

In the general election of 2010, the first-ever televised debates took place in the UK. All the party leaders approached them with trepidation, desperate not to appear an idiot. Afterwards, most pundits and pollsters agreed that Nick Clegg won those debates hands down. Now, there were many reasons why Clegg came out on top: first, he was not as well known as David Cameron and Gordon Brown so had the advantage of looking the freshest; second, he represented the centrist party – an optimum point in persuasion – representing the fulcrum; but, third, and most pertinently, he was the only one of the three leaders who went out of his way to align himself to the audience – showing he was on their side, not against them.

When Nick Clegg looked straight down the eye of the television camera and assured viewers, before anything else, that he understood how they felt, he was speaking squarely and clearly to their instinctive minds. And he was saying, 'I am with you. The others are against you. You are safe with me.'

Our survival instincts naturally draw us towards people who we perceive to be on our side. This protects us from danger, guides us to safety. And what easier way to show we are on someone's side than to say we are on their side? That is why empathy is such an important element in the Language of Leadership.

The most important person in the world is the person you are talking to

When we empathise with people, we create a beautiful chemical reaction in their brain. We get oxytocin flowing. Oxytocin is the love drug. Mothers exude oxytocin when they are breastfeeding. Oxytocin creates an unforgettable sense of connection. The need to connect with others is one of the most motivating forces in the human spirit – as I've mentioned, it's safety in numbers – so, if leaders can get the oxytocin flowing, they are well on the way to creating a loyal band of supporters.

A recent study asked students to research a person from history. Half of the students were told that the person they were researching shared their birth date, the other half were not. The differences in effort and performance between the two groups was staggering. Those who believed that the historical figure shared their birth date spent 65% longer on the research than those who didn't. So don't underestimate the power of connection. When people feel a personal connection, they work 65% harder.[1]

When people feel a personal connection, they work 65% harder

But you can't connect with people unless you understand them.

Empathy

We're not born with the ability to understand others. When we are first born, there is only one view of the world that matters: our own. Scientists think that the ability to understand and appreciate different perspectives kicks in at the age of four. At this point, children use their understanding of different perspectives to make judgements and influence the people around them:

> One way to test a child's capacity for empathy comes from performing a simple puppet show to children. One puppet called Fred hides a biscuit under a cushion and then leaves. Then another puppet called Clara comes in, lifts up the cushion and takes the biscuit, puts it in a basket and leaves. Then Fred comes back. At this point, ask the children where Fred will look for the biscuit. Young children will say the basket, because they will not be able to comprehend that Fred does not know everything that Clara knows. Older children (over four, say) will understand that Fred will not know where it is and will say the cushion.

Some are better at empathy than others. Some have what is known as mindblindness: an inability to appreciate others' perspectives.[2] I once heard about one leader who, in the midst of laying off hundreds of factory workers, said: 'You think you've got problems? I've got five kids at private school!' That's a terminal case of mindblindness.

Simon Baron-Cohen has developed an online tool for checking where you are on the spectrum. You can test your own empathy skills at: http://psychology-tools.com/empathy-quotient/. You just have to answer a series of questions. I scored 52/80. Why not give it a go and see how you do? Great leaders need to understand different perspectives because, without that insight, they're going to find it hard to win people over.

The most effective minister I ever worked with in Whitehall was Alan Johnson. Many people said he should have gone for the top job. With characteristic humility, he said he'd rather be known as the best prime minister we never had than that 'bloody disaster Johnson'. I spent thousands of hours in meetings with him over the years, watching him negotiating between all sorts of people on all sorts of issues. I remember the intense concentration that would fall on his face during these negotiations: his eyes would thin, his brow would furrow and he would repeat people's positions to them, often word for word. When we came out of those meetings, he could summarise everyone's viewpoints word-perfectly. He could also see where to find a deal that worked for everyone. He could do a deal on anything: he was the man who won the debate on introducing university tuition fees in England (this was actually a joint charm offensive with Charles Clarke although, as some said, Johnson was charming and Clarke was offensive).

Effective empathy starts with listening

Listening is underrated as a leadership technique. As the old adage goes, we have two ears and one mouth and we should use them in that proportion. But good listening is harder than it seems.

Listening is underrated as a leadership technique

I sometimes ask my clients if I can record our meetings. It's something I find crucial for really understanding their position. Amidst all the digressions and diversions that naturally take place in the course of any conversation, it can be easy to miss the nuances: it is often only during a second or third listen to a recording that these really begin to emerge. A first listen often only provides a superficial level of understanding.

I know I'm not alone in this. I've often tested very famous speeches on large groups of people: you would be amazed at the massive differences in interpretation that are reached and the huge chunks of text that are seemingly completely unheard. It's a basic flaw in human communication: most of the time when we are listening, we are more wrapped up in our own thoughts than we are with the ideas of the person speaking.

Don't worry if this sounds like you. Help is at hand. There are off-the-shelf models you can use to improve your powers of listening. One model that works well, if you like this kind of thing, is known as CARESS. The CARESS method is shown in Table 5.1.

If this model doesn't work for you, my quick and easy advice is this: put yourself in the other person's shoes. Shut yourself down. Turn off your own judgements, opinions and reactions. Imagine it is you who is saying

TABLE 5.1 The CARESS model

Concentrate	Shut out background noise. Shut down your own ideas. Focus on the speaker.
Acknowledge	Make eye contact and acknowledge what the speaker is saying, including repeating back to them.
Research	Ask questions and provide cues to encourage the person you are speaking to continue.
Emotional control	Contain and control your own reactions to what is being said. Allow them to continue their point.
Sense	Sense the non-verbal messages. Watch the body language to see which are the points that really matter.
Structure	Hear the pattern of the argument that they are making. Try to visualise it, maybe as a mind map.

what they are saying. As Harper Lee wrote in *To Kill a Mockingbird*, 'You never really understand a person... until you climb inside of his skin and walk around in it.' So try to do that. If they are a particularly odious character and you find the idea of inhabiting their skin completely repugnant, don't worry: you can leap out of their skin afterwards. But putting yourself in their shoes whilst they are speaking will help you to develop an empathy and compassion that is natural and authentic and will help to establish you as a leader.

Playing back

Once we understand someone's position, we can play it back. People love to have their own views replayed. We have a deep need to be heard and understood, particularly when that understanding comes from someone we admire and respect – a leader. It gets the oxytocin and the serotonin circulating.

People love having their own views replayed

Just the other day I saw an American from the Deep South make a powerful speech to an audience that had, at first, shown signs of being hostile. She began with total empathy: putting herself completely in the shoes of her audience. 'I know you're angry. I know you expected better from us. I know you're feeling worried about what the future might hold for you and your families. I know you have bills to pay, mouths to feed, commitments to meet...' She went on in this vein for a couple of minutes. Then, having successfully positioned herself alongside her audience she earned the right to make the case in her own defence. But she would not have been entitled to this if she had not started with empathy. It's about breaking down that instinctive hostility and building an alliance.

Another way to strengthen this alliance is through use of the first-person plural. I mentioned this a little earlier but here's the stat: Barack Obama uses the first-person plural (we, us, our) more than twice as frequently as the first-person singular (I, me, mine). What's more, he tends only to use the first-person singular when he has no choice, for instance, when he is talking about his wife or his kids or he is taking personal responsibility for something. This small tweak has a huge impact on the way his language feels.

Just try saying to a large group of people, 'You all have to save more money' and see how it goes. It seems hectoring and haranguing. However, if you say, 'We all have to save more money', then that feels fine. Incidentally, if you disagree and think the first version is better, let me offer a word of advice: *never* go into politics. *Ever*.

'We' is one of the most powerful words in the Language of Leadership: one of the easiest ways to win people over is to use 'we' instead of 'me'. Former US Labour Secretary, Robert B. Reich, once said he used to gauge the health of companies with the 'pronoun' test. Do they talk about the company as 'they' or 'we'?[3] It is a joke amongst speechwriters. One of the easiest ways to make a combative speech more consensual is to spread it out on the floor and then 'we' all over it.

Gender and empathy

Empathy is a skill that some might associate more readily with women. It is true that the part of the brain associated with empathy is usually more enlarged in women than men, but there are exceptions: you can find men who are highly empathetic just as you can also find women who suffer the most infuriating mindblindness. However, as a general trend, that is right.

One interesting piece of research I stumbled across looked at differences in the way that men and women instinctively respond to stress. We often talk about 'fight or flight' but neurologists talk about a further possible response to stress: 'tend and befriend'.

In 26 out of 28 scenarios, women opted for 'tend and befriend' instead of 'fight or flight' in response to stress.[4] I guess this means that, in Neanderthal days, if the man was focused on seeing off some threat, the woman would turn to look after the family. This still rings true with me. A couple of years ago, I was at home with my family, playing upstairs in the kids' bedroom when suddenly we heard a huge crash downstairs: the sound of a window smashing. I quickly grabbed the first weapon-like object I could find (Lottie's Buzz Lightyear doll… Yes, I know! Fat lot of good that would have done…) and went downstairs to find out what was going on. Lucy's response was to huddle up with the children on the floor. When I got downstairs, I discovered a pigeon had flown through the window… but you see how, at a point of stress, the old instincts kicked in?

Empathy is a good trait in a leader. Whether you are naturally empathetic or not, it is a trait you should try to develop. Everyone has a strong need to feel connected. When people feel connected, they feel great. If they feel excluded, the reaction can be fury. We see this fury in some arguments ('WHY CAN'T YOU JUST LISTEN!'). We see it in some political speeches, with leaders slow-handclapped, booed or even physically assaulted (search on YouTube to see the amounts of times leaders have been assaulted by flying shoes during speeches – it is a shockingly common occurrence). We also see it in some pointless so-called 'engagement sessions'. There's no shortage of examples of these: 'engagement session' is now practically a euphemism for a rubber-stamping exercise. But possibly the worst example was when the president of the National Rifle Association called a press conference after the Sandy Hook Massacre and said, 'This is the beginning of a serious conversation. We won't be taking any questions.'[5]

So try to find points of connection, even when you disagree. If you can do this then you can bring a little joy to people's lives. Who knows – you might even put a smile on their face.

chapter

Smiles and Humour

'Let us always meet each other with a smile. Because a smile is the beginning of love.'

Mother Teresa

In September 2014, world leaders descended upon Newport in South Wales for a NATO summit. During a break in proceedings, David Cameron and Barack Obama went to visit a local school. Footage of this was broadcast around the world. I watched it on *BBC News*. The interviewer went up to one of the schoolgirls and asked what the president and the prime minister had said. She replied: 'They didn't say very much. They just smiled.'

I thought this was very telling. Smiles are an essential element in the Language of Leadership. Smiles attract. Smiles relax. Smiles activate the happy, emotional part of the brain.[1] Smiles make us smile. Research shows that it is very hard to look at someone who is smiling and not smile back.[2]

It is hard to look at someone who is smiling and not smile back

That's why a great smile can be the making of a great leader. They smile and it makes people around them feel great. It makes them warm to the

96

leader. It makes them want to give something back: this is why David Frost's smiley interviews always garnered far deeper insights than Jeremy Paxman's hostile hectoring.

Laughter

If smiling is the mark of a good leader, then the ability to tell a gag is the sign of a great leader.

Humour was considered a top attribute for leaders in a survey of Fortune 500 Directors.[3] Humour helps to close sales:[4] research showed that throwing in a little gag at the end of a negotiation ('well, my final offer is $6000 and I'll throw in my pet frog') made it much more likely that a deal would be struck. Humour also breaks down boundaries between divided groups of people.

The role of humour in healing social tensions is well-established.[5] Laughter is, in fact, primarily a social act.[6] This is why we're 30 times more likely to laugh in a social situation than we are when we are alone.[7] If you want to test this, just go to Borders and read a joke book. I bet you don't laugh out loud. Go down the pub, hear someone tell the same jokes and the chances are you'll be falling about on the floor. So when people write LOL on Facebook, they're not really laughing out loud. A more truthful acronym would be AAA: appreciation and acknowledgement.

Laughter emerges from the instinctive brain. It is great for our health: it promotes the release of antibodies, suppresses stress hormones and makes us live longer. The sad thing is that, as we get older, we laugh about four times less often as we did when we were young. So people are really indebted to the leader who puts a smile on their face.

This is not about leaders strolling around guffawing, like Sid James telling smutty jokes that end with 'and it was the milkman'. It is about creating the kind of environment in which people feel relaxed and free from tension.

Managing tension

A little dollop of irreverence can help overcome the awkwardness there is in us having leaders in today's supposedly egalitarian age. Many leaders use humour very deliberately to pop their own bubbles. They tell self-deprecatory gags. Table 6.1 shows some time-honoured examples of self-deprecating gags used by various professions.

Don't go too far with the self-deprecation. You still need to maintain respect. The deprecation should be light: just enough to show you have a sense of humour. You don't *really* want to remind people about your most unattractive traits. There's a thin line between self-deprecation and self-defecation.

Humour can be a great way to diffuse anxiety. It's physically impossible for people to be stressed when they laugh. Doctors, nurses, paramedics, fire officers and police officers all know this. Humour helps them manage the anxiety of their work, creating social cohesion and warmth. I was once

TABLE 6.1   Self-deprecating jokes

Politician	When I told my mother I wanted to go into politics she urged me not to. She said she'd looked it up in the dictionary and it said, 'poly', meaning more than one, and 'tics', which means blood-sucking insects.
Ambassador	One of my predecessors received a call one year from *Time* magazine asking him what he wanted for Christmas. He gave the standard answer: that it would be inappropriate for an ambassador to request anything at all from a publication. The journalist persisted until, finally, the ambassador relented and asked for the smallest gift he could imagine. The next issue of *Time* magazine came out with the feature – 'What world leaders want for Christmas'. It featured Nelson Mandela – freedom for the people of South Africa; Mother Teresa – peace on earth; Her Majesty's Ambassador – a small box of crystallised fruit, please.
Economist	An economist, a biologist and an architect were arguing about what was God's real profession. The biologist said, 'God created man and woman and all living things so clearly he was a biologist.' 'Wrong', said the architect. 'Before that, he created the heavens and the earth. Before the earth, there was only complete confusion and chaos.' 'Well,' said the economist, 'who do you think it was that created chaos and confusion in the first place?'

a guest at a largely Jewish dinner party when close Jewish friends told some shockingly sick jokes about the Holocaust. It was only afterwards that I realized that this was their way of dealing with the horror that their ancestors had suffered. The laughter put them at ease.

This is one of the reasons why Churchill's jokes worked so well: he was prime minister during Britain's darkest days. The war was a time of very serious danger for Britain. How the British people must have loved it when the story spread about Churchill's private secretary knocking on the toilet door to bring him up to date with the latest news on Hitler, only for the prime minister to reply with the immortal line, 'Hold on! I can only deal with one shit at a time!'

Humour can extinguish some very awkward issues. Tony Blair's last party conference as leader of the Labour Party was almost completely thrown off course after a journalist reported that Blair's wife had made derogatory comments about Gordon Brown. Blair quipped that at least he didn't have to worry about his wife running off with the bloke next door. Everyone laughed.

Ronald Reagan also used humour after he was shot in 1981. As he was wheeled into the operating theatre at the George Washington University Hospital, he looked around bleary eyed at the team of clinicians surrounding him. 'I hope you're all Republicans', he said. His chief surgeon replied, 'Mr President, we're all Republicans today.'

Relaxation

Leaders can also tell jokes to put themselves at ease. Here are three tried and tested jokes that have been successfully putting speakers at ease for years:

> There's a story about the Roman gladiator Androcles, who had quite a reputation for staying alive. As many times as he was thrown to the lions, he would return alive. Just as the lion approached Androcles, the gladiator would whisper in his ear, and then the lion would whimper and

retreat. Finally, the Roman emperor called him to his court. 'Androcles,' he said, 'I can take it no longer. I need to know your secret.' 'It's simple, your highness,' Androcles said, 'I just tell him that when he has finished dinner, he'll be asked to say a few words.'

According to most studies, people's number one fear is public speaking. Death is number two. This means that the average person at a funeral would sooner be in the casket than delivering the eulogy.

I'm told a speech should be like a woman's skirt; long enough to cover the subject but short enough to create a bit of interest.

I've seen these jokes used literally dozens of times. They always make people laugh, even if they've heard them before. Do use them if you want, or, if not, find your own jokes to have ready up your sleeve. Many leaders have two or three extremely well-rehearsed jokes that they use again and again at receptions, dinner parties and at the beginning of speeches. *Bartlett's Book of Anecdotes* is filled with gems.

Every great leader should have a joke at the ready. Even Gordon Brown had a joke that he would tell on special occasions. Here it is, preserved for posterity:

> In the 1980s, Olof Palme, the Prime Minister of Sweden, visited Washington for a bilateral meeting with President Reagan. When Reagan was told he was meeting him, he said, 'Isn't that man a communist?' 'No, Mr President. He's an anti-communist', replied his Chief of Staff. To which Reagan said, 'I don't care what kind of communist he is, get him out of here!'

The secrets of a good joke

So what makes a good joke? A lot of research has been carried out into this question: but before I share the findings, I should warn you that dissecting jokes is a bit like dissecting frogs – you may learn more about them but you will inevitably kill them in the process. So, if you want to maintain the mystery, I suggest you flick to the next chapter now.

Research has shown that jokes are most likely to make us laugh if they are 103 words long; the funniest animals to make jokes about are ducks; and jokes are funniest if they are told at 6.03 in the evening. Some research showed the funniest joke in the world to be this:[8]

> Two hunters are out in the woods when one of them collapses. He doesn't seem to be breathing and his eyes are glazed. The other guy whips out his phone and calls the emergency services. He gasps, 'My friend is dead! What can I do?' The operator says, 'Calm down. I can help. First, let's make sure he's dead.' There is a silence. Then a shot is heard. The guy picks up the phone again and says, 'Okay. Now what?'

Experts say that there are two ingredients to a funny joke: surprise and superiority. Surprise at the punchline (which releases dopamine); superiority because the joke is at someone else's expense (which releases serotonin).

There are two ingredients to a funny joke: surprise and superiority

The point about superiority is worth emphasising: some leaders think it is funny to make themselves look superior at the expense of their audience. It is not. People will consider them cruel. It is much safer to tell self-deprecatory jokes that place the leader as the butt of the joke. It gives the audience a sense of superiority.

Another way to create this feeling of superiority is by picking on someone outside of the room. Many British leaders make jokes about the French. For instance, there's a funny, but almost certainly apocryphal story about a French politician who was delivering a speech in the European Parliament. He kept talking about the 'sagacity of the French' (*la sagacité Normand*), but every time he did so the British delegation burst out laughing. He kept repeating the phrase, but every time he repeated it, the British delegation laughed again. It turned out that the interpreters had been saying, 'Norman Wisdom... Norman Wisdom...'

Attacking other groups of people may get a laugh but it can backfire if it gets back to the target of the gag. This is what happened when Andy Street, managing director of John Lewis, made some off-the-cuff jokes about the French that were picked up by the media. The French prime minister was wonderfully dismissive: 'Perhaps he had drunk too much beer.'[9] Ouch.

Set-up and payoff

The basic structure of a joke is two-step: set-up and payoff, as shown in Table 6.2.

The basic structure of a joke is two-step: set-up and payoff

The thing that all of the jokes in Table 6.2 have in common is that the payoff comes *literally* in the last word. It is at that point that the dopamine is released, so that's when we get the hit. That's why the delivery of the punchline is so important. Getting the pause right between the end of the set-up and the payoff is the magic of 'comic timing'. With shaggy dog stories, people really play with the distance between set-up and payoff. It often feels like a man with a bow and arrow, pulling back the bow – back, back, back – and then piaoooow!

The rule of three can enhance the effect in humour because it increases our sense of expectation. Once people recognize the three-part structure of the joke they are poised for the punchline. That is why the rule of three features so frequently. 'Infamy, infamy, they've all got it in for me' was voted the funniest line in movie history. And, of course, what of the 'Englishman, Irishman, Scotsman' jokes – where are the Welsh? The Welsh are omitted because adding a fourth would disrupt the rhythm.

TABLE 6.2 **Set-up and payoff of jokes**

Set-up	Payoff
For 18 years, my husband and I were the happiest people in the world...	Then we met.
Did you hear about the Brummie soldier who got stationed in Iraq...	He kept getting flashbacks to being in Birmingham.
Never pick a fight with an ugly person.	They've got nothing to lose.
A pompous young minister once called himself 'we' in the presence of Edward VII. Edward VII said that only two people can do that. A queen...	And a man with a tapeworm.

Testing jokes

There are few worse fates that can befall a leader than a duff joke. There have been a few times in my life when I've seen the tumbleweed roll and I can tell you: it's not pleasant. Avoid this at all costs. The good news is that there is a very easy way to test jokes. Try them out and check if people laugh. If so, it works. If not, dump it. And, when I say laugh, I mean really laugh. An involuntary laugh. Not a forced laugh to be polite. Be sure their laugh was genuine. It should take their breath away – which takes us to the next chapter.

chapter **7**

Breathing

Every parent has a childcare secret they proudly share with anyone who wants to listen, so here's mine: when my daughters were babies and going through the inevitable sleepless nights, I had a little technique to turn them from screaming banshees to gorgeous Buddhas in minutes. I held them tightly to my chest and deliberately imitated their breathing. Then I slowed it down. As my chest pressed out, so would theirs; before long our breathing would sync. We'd be breathing in harmony.

People naturally tune in to the breathing of those around them – particularly those in authority. It's a survival mechanism: a way to assess their environment and check they are safe, gauging the moods of those around them. Fairly sensible, isn't it? After all, if someone near you is hyperventilating, there is probably a good reason why you should be hyperventilating too – maybe you need to run, hide or take evasive action. That's why our breathing patterns instinctively transfer.

People naturally tune in to the breathing of those around them

But, because we connect with each other in this way, breathing also provides a simple and powerful way for leaders to influence and lead the mood. They can do so in two extreme ways, depending on the mood they want to create. Short, sharp breathing causes anxiety. Deep, steady breaths can imbue a deep and powerful sense of calm. Both are effective: people are more receptive to persuasion when they are either highly anxious or deeply relaxed.[1] Using your breathing to lead others is another secret of the Language of Leadership.

Super-short sentences – anxious and edgy

People naturally speak in short sentences when they are anxious. They can't help it. It's their instinctive brain. Sucking in oxygen. Preparing to fight. Ready to run. So their breathing speeds up, they hyperventilate and, consequently, they struggle to get their words out.

You see this happen authentically if you watch someone being interviewed on Sky News immediately after witnessing some terrible disaster. The people being interviewed invariably speak in incredibly short sentences. 'It was terrible. There was a bang. Flash. People started running. It was terrifying.' They are literally winded by the experience, struggling to catch their breath.

Likewise, when abuse victims describe their experiences, the recollection of the past trauma can cause them to speak in short sentences. 'I felt guilty. Responsible. Like it was my fault. Dirty. Ashamed.' Short sentences like these are the natural manifestation of the physical state of panic.

Leaders who want to create a sense of anxiety will also sound breathless. By contriving a sense of panic, they can transfer that mood to others. This is something that great leaders have done throughout the ages. It is an ancient rhetorical device. The Romans called these breathless short sentences 'asyndeton' and it is still around today. Many of Tony Blair's earliest soundbites were based on asyndeton. 'New Labour. New Britain.' 'The party renewed. The country reborn.' David Cameron also uses it: 'Broken homes. Failing schools. Sink estates.' This is scripted breathlessness.

Some leaders actually force themselves into such a state that they are genuinely breathless. If you want to watch a hilarious example of this, watch the YouTube video of Steve Balmer, then Microsoft's CEO, whipping up a Microsoft sales conference by running around the stage. He gets himself completely out of breath. But the crowd goes crazy. He's leading. You can watch it here: https://www.youtube.com/watch?v=wvsboPUjrGc.

There are other techniques: it is said that Enoch Powell avoided going to the toilet before making a speech – another ancient Roman practice – to ensure he projected the right sense of urgency in his speeches (this sounds like a good strategy, but it is probably high risk as you get older).

In one of my favourite episodes of *The West Wing*, Jed Bartlett's team are worried he is looking too complacent just before he goes into a presidential debate. So, ten seconds before he's due on stage, Abby Bartlett takes out a pair of scissors and cuts his tie in half. The president is incensed. Furious. He goes bright red and starts hyperventilating. Another tie is produced. His staff quickly push him out on to the stage. He's angry. He's passionate. He's hyperventilating. *Now* he's ready to perform.

Super-long sentences – relaxed and confident

Where short sentences induce anxiety, long sentences imbue a deep sense of calm. Barack Obama can merrily reel off 30-plus words whilst barely drawing breath. He's got the most amazing set of lungs. His breath shows his exceptional strength but also his extraordinary confidence, like a lion letting out a long sleepy yawn. Speaking at this rate keeps Obama calm, but it also spreads calm all around.

Short sentences induce anxiety, long sentences imbue a deep sense of calm

This is great, but we can't always contrive such calm. Sometimes when we are trying desperately to appear calm, our breathing can betray us.

Our breathing can betray us

I recently worked with someone who was given the unenviable job of going around the world closing down national offices for a big global corporation. He was usually a confident leader but he found that, during these large meetings, confronted with 250 people or so who were losing their jobs, his breath would speed up and he became anxious. It's easy to see how this happened. His instinctive mind sensed danger, so fight or flight kicked in and his breath quickened. The trouble was that this made him appear confrontational, which made the people he was talking to feel even more edgy. So the situation he was trying to extinguish escalated. We worked on his breathing so that he could calm situations like this in future.

There are a number of great trainers who work with leaders to improve their breathing. I sometimes run my Language of Leadership workshops alongside trainers who specialise in yoga: the effects can be astonishing in terms of renewed focus and togetherness. One trainer who I have worked with for a number of years with great results can be found at www.calmercorporation.co.uk. But here are some quick tips to help you along.

The first thing to do to help control your breathing is to make sure you exhale through your nose, not your mouth. When people exhale through their mouth it makes them sound breathless and unwell, like Tony Soprano stumbling around in the later episodes of *The Sopranos*.

The second thing is to make sure you are breathing from your diaphragm, which is at the very base of your stomach, just above your pelvic bone. You can do exercises to strengthen your diaphragm and there are plenty of videos on YouTube showing you how to do this. It's good to do: not just to help with your speaking, but also because it improves your posture and help you feel better about yourself. I occasionally do these exercises myself: it feels like a drag beforehand but I always feel great afterwards.

Breathing in writing

Mimicking extreme breathing patterns is not just a device for the spoken word, it can prove equally powerful in the written word. When people read, a little voice in their head usually vocalises everything anyway, so these techniques can have a similar effect. Plus, people are now increasingly writing in a conversational style. Asyndeton can also prove very effective in advertising. I recently saw a billboard ad for rightmove.com that demonstrated asyndeton beautifully: 'On the market, off the market, that sold fast, open the champers'.

That example is less about breathing per se than it is about the *style* of writing, which takes us on seamlessly to the next element of the Language of Leadership.

chapter

8 Style

'Through the style, we find the man'

Ancient Roman saying

Style is substance

Cabinet reshuffles are an exciting time in Whitehall. As speechwriter to a cabinet minister, you never know whether the boss is going to move; nor can you be sure that, if they do move, they're going to invite you along with them. In 2007, I moved with Alan Johnson when he was shuffled from the Department of Education to the Department of Health. Instantly there were a number of major speeches and parliamentary statements to write. I was plunged head first into a series of meetings to acquaint me with the issues. These meetings were horrendous. Everyone spoke this awful jargon. Everyone was constantly saying words like benchmarking, collaborating, beacons, deliverables, frameworks. I emerged from one of these meetings and said to the official beside me, someone who had been working at the department for years: 'I didn't understand a word of that.' 'Oh!' she said. 'Thank God! I thought it was just me!'

The way we speak and write sends all sorts of instinctive messages about who we are and where we come from. Some make the mistake of thinking that convoluted jargon enhances their leadership credentials. It does not. In fact, people who are on the receiving end invariably find it alienating and unhelpful: the measure of success for any language must be its effect on its audience so, by that measure, it fails. But also it fails as an expression of leadership.

Research was carried out a few years ago by the then HM Customs and Excise. A sample group of members of the public were shown two letters: one was full of jargon with long words and long sentences; the other was brief, jargon-free and to the point. The readers of the letters were then asked to guess the seniority of the author of each letter. Overwhelmingly, recipients believed that the brief letter had come from a senior person in the organisation whilst believing that the convoluted letter had come from someone more junior.

The insight is this: we expect our leaders to speak in plain English. Leaders have clear visions and they present them in clear language. Leaders are confident enough to speak clearly without fear. In contrast, people who are insecure about their status are likely to seek refuge in overly elaborate language: a bit like those wonderfully verbose entries in Adrian Mole's diary after he had bought his thesaurus – they are fearful of challenge.

I spend a lot of my time analysing people's language and one feature I have repeatedly noticed is how non-native English speakers habitually use longer words and sentences than native English speakers. I have also found that social status also appears to have a bearing: in a study I carried out on political language in 2010, the three politicians who spoke with the shortest sentences all went to private schools whilst the politicians with the lengthiest sentences were all state-educated. The difference between the two was startling: the sentences were as much as three times as long.

I took from this that people who felt they had something to prove had subconsciously revealed they had something to prove. So the insight here is simple: if you feel you have something to prove, speak as if you have nothing to prove. Or, to put it even more simply, as the old advice goes: keep it simple, stupid (KISS).

Speak as if you have nothing to prove

The good, the bad and the ugly

Every week, most of us receive hundreds of emails. We can't read them all and we don't read them all. Instead, our instinctive mind filters on our behalf, sifting like a brilliant PA, automatically guiding us towards some emails whilst leading us away from others. Style has a critical bearing on these judgements.

Take a look at the two emails below that recently arrived in my inbox. In some ways they are similar: both come from global companies (Facebook and Vodafone) and both were sent to each of those company's entire customer base. The styles, however, are extremely different. Which would you rather read?

This is the email from Facebook:

> We recently announced some proposed updates to our Data Use Policy, which explains how we collect and use data when people use Facebook, and our Statement of Rights and Responsibilities (SRR), which explains the terms governing use of our services.
>
> The updates provide you with more detailed information about our practices and reflect changes to our products including:
>
> * New tools for managing your Facebook Messages;
> * Changes on how we refer to certain products;
> * Tips on managing your timeline; and
> * Reminders about what's visible to other people
>
> We are also proposing changes to our site governance process for future updates to our Data Use Policy and SRR. We deeply value the feedback we receive from you during our comment period but have found the voting mechanism created a system that incentivised quantity of comments over the quality of them. So we are proposing to end the voting component in order to promote a more meaningful environment for feedback. We also plan to roll out new engagement channels, including a feature for submitting questions about privacy to our Chief Privacy Officer of Policy.
>
> We encourage you to review these proposed changes and give us feedback.

No hello. No goodbye. And this email was sent by Facebook to every single one of their customers. As you might imagine, it didn't go down too well. Within minutes of the email being issued, the internet was buzzing with conspiracy theories as everyone tried to decipher what the hell all this terrible jargon actually meant. Trust in Facebook was never particularly high but it fell further in the aftermath of that email.

Contrast that with this email from Vodafone:

> Hello Simon
>
> This month's bill for account number ending 6625 is ready online. It's for £91.20.
>
> If it's a bit more than usual, it could be because you went over the minutes, texts or data included in your plan. Or made calls to '08' or international numbers. Or even used your phone abroad.
>
> You'll find more about what is and isn't included in your plan on your bill. And there are some great ways to keep costs down at Vodafone. co.uk/extras.
>
> Best regards
>
> Vodafone Customer Services team

Look at that. Much better. And this email could have been much more difficult – my bill with Vodafone has consistently been higher than I expected, but because they write so nicely, it is hard to get too cross. I feel like Vodafone is my friend (I know, I'm a sucker).

You almost certainly have examples of the good, the bad and the ugly lurking in your own inbox. Have a look. See what works and what doesn't. Scribble down the attributes that you most admire. Develop your own style guide to show what works for you.

These are some of the things that work for me:

- short words;
- short sentences;

- informal style;
- keeping it simple;
- one idea per sentence;
- active voice;
- avoiding adverbs and adjectives.

Curiously, as I was editing the final draft of this book, Facebook sent me another email – another one to all their customers. They've come a long way. Look at this:

> Hi Simon,
>
> We wanted to let you know we're updating our terms and policies on January 1, 2015 and introducing Privacy Basics. You can check out the details below or on Facebook.
>
> Over the past year, we've introduced new features and controls to help you get more out of Facebook, and listened to people who have asked us to better explain how we get and use information.
>
> Now, with Privacy Basics, you'll get tips and a how-to guide for taking charge of your experience on Facebook. We're also updating our terms, data policy and cookies policy to reflect new features we've been working on and to make them easy to understand. And we're continuing to improve ads based on the apps and sites you use off Facebook and expanding your control over the ads you see.
>
> We hope these updates improve your experience. Protecting people's information and providing meaningful privacy controls are at the core of everything we do and we believe today's announcement is an important step.
>
> Sincerely, Erin Egan
>
> Global Chief Privacy Officer.

Isn't that much better? Shorter words. None of those awful metaphors. And even a signature at the end. It's as if they read my mind…

If you want to get some insights into your own style, there is a range of online resources you can use. You can check your readability at

www.usingenglish.com. You can check your average word and
sentence length at wordcalc.org. The main point, though, is
don't be afraid to simplify your style. Don't worry about
dumbing down. The simpler and more accessible your
language, the more likely you are to win people over.
Comprehension is the essential entry point to any communication. And the trends are only headed one way. A study
showed that Barack Obama's vocabulary is the simplest of any president in
history… And some people have criticised him for being too intellectual.

Don't worry about dumbing down

There are all sorts of other elements of our style that can influence how we
are perceived. There are some stylistic devices that can set warning lights
flashing. Curious to know more? Well, scientists at Edinburgh University
analysed emails and found certain features that were typically associated
with neuroses:[1] for instance, a more erratic use of commas and adverbs,
beginning sentences with the word 'well' and multiple exclamation marks
or quotation marks???!! Of course, fonts also convey a message. One of
my old friends used to send emails in size 26 fluorescent Comic Sans font.
I'm not quite sure what she was thinking but I always imagined she was
in the midst of a nasty acid trip. A nice, healthy Arial 12 never did anyone
any harm.

These may seem like minor matters but they all play their part. They all
subtly influence the perception people have of us as a leader. Another
thing that influences that view is our names, so that is what we look at
next in the Language of Leadership.

9

chapter

What's in a Name?

'The naming of cats is a difficult matter, it isn't just one of your holiday games.'

T.S. Eliot

The other night, Lucy and I were in a restaurant. When the waitress came over to tell us our table was ready, a couple nearby heard our name was Lancaster and instantly came over to strike up conversation. They were also Lancasters – a couple of generations older – and we then chatted throughout the evening, swapping notes on the Lancasters of the north of England, the Lancasters in Wales, the Lancasters in London and beyond. The oxytocin was flowing… There was no blood tie between us but we bonded through little more than our names.

Here's the insight. Our names are very special to us and our instinctive mind instinctively pulls us towards people with the same name. We love our own names. We also love the letters, sounds and syllables within our names.

It seems bonkers but there's heaps of research on this topic. Research shows we are more likely to marry people whose names include the same sounds as ours: my initials are SL – my wife's name is Lucy. Research shows we are more likely to buy brands that include sounds in our name – the last major product I bought was a Samsung TV.[1] And research shows that people are more likely to carry out professions that have an alliterative match to our own names[2] (in my early career, I tried my hand as a singer, songwriter, salesperson and civil servant, before finally landing up as a speechwriter).

So our names can discreetly affect our path in life. Academics refer to this using the charming term 'nominative determinism', and there are some hilarious examples of it in practice: Usain *Bolt* is the fastest sprinter in history. Until last year Justice Igor *Judge* was the most senior judge in the UK. And, one of the first-ever articles in the *New Statesman* on urology was penned by a Dr A.J. *Splatt* and Dr D. *Weedon*.[3] Bet they made a real splash.

Shaping our own names

A leader's name influences that crucial first impression. Whether I describe myself as Mr Lancaster, S. Lancaster, Simon Lancaster, Si Lancaster or Simon John Lancaster sends slight messages: not huge, but every little counts.

So are you a Christopher or a Chris, a Samantha or a Sam? You never know: it might just make a difference. Could Steve Jobs have ever made it as Steven Jobs? Would Richard Branson have been such a loveable legend if he had been known as Dicky? What signs does your name send?

Increasingly, leaders today express their name in the simplest form possible. Just 50 years ago, Nick Clegg, Ed Balls and Ed Miliband would almost certainly have been known in public as Nicholas Clegg, Edward Balls and Edward Miliband. The shortened name makes them more approachable.

Leaders today express their name in the simplest form possible

It was Anthony Wedgwood-Benn who started this trend when he forfeited his hereditary peerage in the 1960s and rebranded himself as Tony Benn. Tony Blair went one step further with his 'Call me

Tony' strategy in government, even though the acerbic columnist Peter Hitchens insisted on continuing to call him Anthony Charles Lynton Blair.

Changing our names

Changing your name might seem quite an extreme step to take, but it has been known. George Osborne changed his name from Gideon when he started out in politics: almost certainly a sensible decision. The truth is that people are judged by their names, people do suffer prejudice and our names do influence how we are perceived. A famous study on 'Harriets' versus 'Harrys' showed that Harrys were far more likely to be perceived as fun types whilst Harriets were regarded as bores.

Some women change their names in order to conceal their gender, such as J.K. Rowling and P.D. James. The decision for many women on whether or not they change their names on marriage is often fraught.

Some people change their name to counter racial prejudice. Research by the Runnymede Trust has shown how people with ethnic-sounding names can be discriminated against in recruitment processes, based on nothing but their name. Yes, we should do all we can to ensure that such discrimination does not take place but, as long as it does, we should use these insights to make sure we come out as winners.

Remembering names

Given the special place our names have in all of our hearts, leaders simply must get people's names right. People visibly flinch when someone forgets or mispronounces their name. That's how much it hurts. In the run-up to the 2015 general election in the UK, Ed Balls was asked on BBC's *Newsnight* to name a businessperson who backed the Labour Party. He replied, 'Bill somebody…'

People visibly flinch when someone forgets or mispronounces their name

I've often been struck by how great leaders work a room, wooing everyone with a seemingly magic ability to remember the names of everyone they meet. It's clearly a Language of Leadership trick. I once asked a politician who did this particularly well for his secret.

He told me: exaggerate one of that person's facial features and find a connection with their name. So, say you were trying to remember my name, you might look at my eyes. Then, in your imagination, grossly enlarge and distort them, and think of me as 'Eyeman'. On a further meeting, the Eyeman memory would return, from which it is only a small step back to Simon.

The first time I tried this technique, I was amazed. I could recall the names of 30 people after a meeting: what's more, this was in Asia, where the names were unfamiliar.

So there concludes Part I of the book: techniques to win over the instinctive brain. It's all about positioning the leader as someone who offers safety and fulfilment. Now, we can move up to the emotional part of the brain and look at how we make people care.

Part II

Winning the Emotional Mind

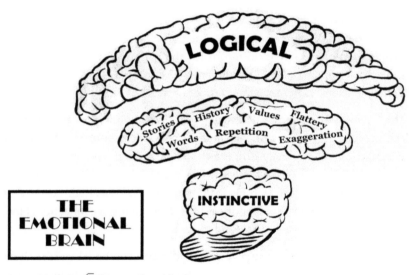

FIGURE PT II.1 / The emotional brain

'Where there is discord, may we bring harmony. Where there is fear, may we bring hope.'

Francis of Assisi

Leadership is based on emotion

When Mike Tyson was a young boy, he was totally out of control. He was so bad that his own mother gave up on him and threw him out. At the tender age of 12, he was living on the streets and already involved in organised crime. But into this crazy picture stepped a white middle-aged man who rescued him. Cus D'Amato took Tyson under his wing, led him away from crime and into boxing. How did he tame him? He did it very simply. He told Tyson he was great. As Mike Tyson wrote in his autobiography:

> I had never heard anyone say nice things about me before. I wanted to stay around this old guy because I liked the way he made me feel. You give a weak man some strength and he becomes addicted.

No one could better explain what it means to find a leader in life. Leadership is an emotional contract. The leader meets people's emotional needs. In return for that, the leader gains their support. Cus D'Amato met Tyson's emotional needs so Tyson made Cus D'Amato his leader.

Leadership is an emotional contract

This is how leaders grow such strong emotional bonds with their followers. Look at Steve Jobs's online condolence book: people who had never met him were completely distraught. See how people around the world wept with joy when Barack Obama was elected. I have friends who travelled from the UK to watch his inauguration: some were so moved that they had the date tattooed on their arms. Now that is a connection. How many leaders could claim that kind of support?

But, of course, different people have different emotional needs. Great leaders know this and respond accordingly. This explains how leaders can prove a bit 'Marmite': some people love them; others hate them. Russell Brand is winning a following for successfully articulating the anger that some feel, but others regard him as a jumped-up joker. On the other side of the coin, people like Obama are offering hope to millions, but he makes some nauseous. Different political parties offer emotional appeals to meet the needs of their natural bases: Labour plays to anger, the Liberal Democrats appeal to pity, the Conservatives stir up pride. We all have different needs.

Once people find the leader who meets their emotional needs, they will go the extra mile for them. They will make sacrifices for them on the promise of emotional fulfilment. They are chasing the drugs: the serotonin, the oxytocin and the dopamine. They are looking to the leader to make them feel confident, to make them feel understood, to make them feel connected. Whatever they need, the leader provides. That is the deal.

But the relationship between the leader and their followers is not permanent and is not unconditional: it is constantly being tested and renewed, and it can be withdrawn at a moment's notice by either side. And when the contract is withdrawn, it can prove traumatic for both sides. At that point, emotions can be plunged into reverse. Hope can turn to anger, pride to shame, passion to hate: look how fierce the criticism of Blair was after the Iraq War. He had started by offering hope and ended by offering fear. The reason he lost his grip as leader was because he stopped meeting people's emotional needs. The force behind that connection was lost. People felt deceived.

Some leaders are wary of connecting emotionally. They are afraid of the risks; they hope they can succeed with logic alone. That is fear. That is their own emotion talking.

The truth is that emotion just can't be ignored – it is a fundamental part of the human condition. Human beings simply are emotional creatures. There is no way around this. Understanding the power of emotion will give you an enormous advantage. In politics, the party that makes the strongest emotional connections wins.[1] In business, the company that makes the strongest emotional connections – with their employees and their customers – wins.[2]

So in this part of the book we take a look around the emotional brain. We look at the chemical reactions that put the fire in the belly and goose pimples on the arms. And one of the simplest ways we can do so is through *story*.

chapter 10

Stories and Emotion

'Tell me a fact and I'll learn. Tell me a truth and I'll believe.
But tell me a story and it will live in my heart forever.'

Native American saying

The power of story

Have you seen the 1980s film *Stand By Me*? If you have, I bet you remember the scene when the kids sit around the campfire, all huddled up, listening intently as Gordie told the story about Davie Hogan: otherwise known as… 'Lardass'. It was a tragic tale. For years, Lardass had been teased and tormented about his weight by everyone in the town. But one day, he hatched a wicked plan for his revenge. He entered the local pie-eating contest. Before taking part in the contest, he swallowed a dozen raw eggs and a whole bottle of castor oil. Soon after eating his first pie, his belly started churning. The more pies he ate, the more ominous rumbling sounds emerged. Finally, as he tucked into his fifth blueberry pie, he could hold back no longer: he barfed all over the place. This made his chief tormentor barf over someone else. Then that person barfed on the mayor's wife. Before long, everyone was barfing. And everyone was barfed upon. It was a barfarama. And Lardass sat back in his chair, satisfied. Justice had been done.

Lots of people remember the scene, but what they remember, more than the details of Lardass's story – fabulous though that is – are the feelings evoked by the campfire scene. It makes them nostalgic for the intimacy and honesty of their own childhood. There is no more powerful symbol of intimacy and honesty than sharing stories.

Everyone enjoys stories and has done so since the dawn of time. Stories are evident in prehistoric cave paintings, ancient myths and fables through to modern dramas, blogs and Facebook statuses. Story is the default mode of human communication. Just listen to a group of friends chatting: it won't be long until a story is swapped: 65% of conversation is based on personal stories and gossip. These stories provide joy but they also serve another purpose: through stories, we learn more about ourselves, each other and our place in the world.

That is why storytelling is part of the Language of Leadership. The storyteller has a natural authority. As children we hear stories from our parents, teachers and elders. Religious, military, political, business and social leaders have been telling stories for thousands of years.

The storyteller has a natural authority

Stories have an awesome effect on the brain. We know this from fMRI.

When people are just chatting (i.e. not telling stories) two parts of the brain come to life: the auditory cortex (concerned with listening) and the Werner's area (concerned with deciphering language). However, when people are listening to stories, the scanner goes crazy. The more active the story, the greater the activity levels shown.

People are actively not passively involved when they are listening to stories.[1] If the protagonist in our story is said to be gripping an object, the motor cortex part of the listener's brain lights up as if they are gripping an object as well. If there is a sad bit in the story, the empathy parts of the brain light up as if they are sad as well. If the story describes a pungent smell in the room, the olfactory senses in the brain light up as if the listener is actually being exposed to a pungent smell. So, with stories, we can create worlds which our listeners really experience.

We also establish a strong sense of connection between storyteller and listener. Uri Hasson from Princeton University compared brain activity between storytellers and story listeners. He found that, as stories are being told, brain activity synchronises between the storyteller and the story listener. So, when we tell stories, people really do see the world through our eyes.

This is what makes stories so memorable. I can still remember stories told to me by my headmaster at school, many years after the event. Research from Stanford University shows that stories are ten times as memorable as statistics.[2] But stories are not just memorable, they are great at winning minds.

Stories are ten times as memorable as statistics

Let me give you an example. Just recently I was at a dinner, sitting next to a powerful woman from the insurance industry. It was bad timing. Just two weeks previously, I had been really let down on our vehicle breakdown insurance policy. I told her the story. We were on our way to the funeral of Maud, one of our lovely old neighbours from Maida Vale in West London, and, on the way there, the car broke down. We were stuck at a service station 120 miles away from where we needed to be. As we rang the helpline for assistance, it became instantly clear that our policy was woefully inadequate. We ended up missing the funeral.

The woman sympathised. She asked if I'd bought the insurance policy as an add-on. I had – it came with my bank account. She sighed. You need to be careful with those policies, she said. Some of the companies offering them were ruthless and the provision was invariably inadequate. Her company was different: they didn't sell add-ons. They charged a little more for their policies but they provided a much better service. She had just heard that day about one of their clients who had recently written off his beloved Ford Capri. He'd been unable to find a replacement and was heartbroken. One of her claims handlers, unperturbed, scoured the classifieds until he tracked down a near-perfect replacement. When they delivered it to the client he was ecstatic.

This was a very typical kind of business lunch conversation, but do you see what happened? Essentially, we were having a little argument. What

I was saying was basically, 'I think the insurance industry is a big rip-off.' What she was saying was basically, 'We're not all that bad.' But, by having the argument through stories, we dealt with our disagreement in a calm, collected way, without a row. This is just one of the things that stories do: they provide a non-confrontational way to settle disputes. Some neuroscientists think that is why stories evolved in the first place: to keep us civil.[3]

Stories serve a number of purposes for leaders. But how do we create a good story that will stick? It's all about the chemicals. Great stories produce oxytocin, cortisol and dopamine.

The secrets of great stories

Let's look a bit closer at how we get these drugs going:

- *Great characters produce oxytocin.* Whether your story is first or second hand, the listener must be able to identify with the lead character: that's what gets the oxytocin going. So make sure there are plenty of sources of identification. Describe what the character is doing, in as sensory a manner as possible – what they can they see, feel and hear – try to put the listener in the character's shoes.[4] This is what they're doing in the movies when they open showing someone driving along the highway singing along with the radio. Everyone's watching thinking, 'Yup. That's me.' Oxytocin.
- *Great dilemmas produce cortisol.* At the heart of every great story lies a dilemma: it is that which creates the force that holds people's attention. It might be an 'us against them' or 'do I do this or do I do that' dilemma – it doesn't really matter, it's creating a source of tension. The set-up of the conflict creates the expectancy of the payoff in resolution.
- *Great resolution produces dopamine.* People are motivated to listen to the end of a story because they want the resolution and the squirt of dopamine that payoff brings. But they won't wait forever. A good story

needs momentum. A German theorist 150 years ago, Gustav Freytag, developed a dramatic arc for great storytelling, comprising five steps: exposition, rising action, climax, falling action and denouement.

As I mentioned earlier, there was a research project where a group was shown a cartoon that told a story about a father's grief, knowing his son was dying of cancer. At the end of the story, the group was asked if they would give some money. The researchers found (i) those who produced cortisol and oxytocin were more likely to give money than those who did not; and (ii) the more cortisol and oxytocin that was produced, the more money they were likely to give. So stories really do change behaviour.

But, a final word of caution: everyone who hears a story takes something slightly different from it. We all have different values and different perspectives: different people can hear exactly the same story but draw fiercely different conclusions.

Recently at a party I heard a terrible story about a young woman who lives not far from me. She had been due to go out with her boyfriend one Saturday night. She was running late. She was just getting out of the shower when the boyfriend pulled up outside and beeped his horn. She still had loads to do: dry her hair, do her make-up, get dressed – so she started to speed up. A few minutes passed and the boyfriend started beeping the horn more, evidently getting angrier. Worried about the neighbours, she sped up even more, squeezing into her high heels and setting off down the steps: but she tripped on the top step, tumbling 15 feet down the stairs and landing on her spinal cord. She will never walk again.

Now Lucy and I have ongoing disagreements about timeliness. We have actually missed flights because we regularly run late. So I told Lucy this story, making a little dig about being on time. I asked her what she thought. She turned to me, sighed, and said, '*Never* hurry.'

11 Personal Stories

'There is no greater agony than bearing an untold story inside you.'

Maya Angelou

When we fall in love, there comes a moment of beautiful connection. It is that special moment when we share something personal and intimate, maybe something we've never told anyone else before: a major story about something in our lives. In the movies, they typically depict this moment taking place atop the Hollywood Hills in a red Cadillac after a night at a funfair.

In a real relationship this moment might be months in the making. Leaders can't wait that long. They need to connect instantly, so they leap straight in. They happily tell complete strangers stories that the rest of us would hesitate to tell our therapists.

Here are three examples of personal stories being told by three different leaders from different fields – business, music and politics:

Jeff Bezos:

As a kid, I spent my summers with my grandparents on their ranch in Texas. I loved and worshipped my grandparents and I really looked forward to these trips.

On one trip, I was about ten years old, rolling around in the big bench seat in the back of the car. My grandfather was driving. And my grandmother had the passenger seat. She smoked throughout these trips, and I hated the smell.

At that age, I'd take any excuse to do minor arithmetic. I'd been hearing an ad campaign about smoking. I can't remember but basically the ad said every puff of a cigarette takes two minutes off your life. I decided to do the maths for my grandmother. I poked my head into the front of the car and proudly proclaimed, 'You've taken nine years off your life!'

I expected to be applauded for my cleverness. Instead, my grandmother burst into tears. I sat in the back seat and did not know what to do. While my grandmother sat crying, my grandfather, who had been driving in silence, pulled over onto the shoulder of the highway. He got out of the car and came around and opened my door and waited for me to follow.

I had no experience in this realm with my grandparents and no way to gauge what the consequences might be. We stopped beside the trailer. My grandfather looked at me. After a bit of silence, he gently and calmly said, 'Jeff, one day you'll understand that it's harder to be kind than clever.'

David Cameron:

When it comes to our elderly, one thing matters above everything. Knowing the NHS is there for you. From Labour last week, we heard the same old rubbish about the Conservatives and the NHS. Spreading complete and utter lies.

I just think: how dare you. It was the Labour Party who gave us the scandal at Mid Staffs… elderly people begging for water and dying of neglect.

For me, this is personal. I am someone who has relied on the NHS – whose family knows more than most how important it is… who knows what it's like to go to hospital night after night with a child in your arms… knowing that when you get there, you have people who will care for that child and love that child like their own.

How dare they suggest I would ever put that at risk for other people's children? How dare they frighten those who are relying on the NHS right now? It might be the only thing that gets a cheer at their party conference but it is frankly pathetic.

Peter Gabriel:

The school I was at had a lot of trees, it had a tulip tree. At the time, I think it was the biggest tulip tree in the country, and it also had a lot of wonderful bushes and vegetation around the playing fields.

One day I was grabbed by some of my classmates. I was taken in the bushes, I was stripped, I was attacked, I was abused and this came out of the blue. Now the reason I say that is that afterwards when I went back into the school I felt dirty, I felt betrayed, I felt ashamed but mainly I felt powerless.

Thirty years later I was sitting on an aeroplane next to a lady called Veronica who came from Chile and we were on a human rights tour and she was telling me what it was like to be tortured and, from my privileged position, this was my only reference point. This was an amazing learning experience because human rights was something I had a bit of an interest in but really it was about something that happened to people who were 'over there'.

These stories are each unique, but they each have the three essential elements of a strong story: identification, stress and resolution. First, we very much experience the narrator's world: we step into their shoes. We can smell the smoke in the back of Jeff Bezos's car, we are dazzled by the bright lights in David Cameron's hospital, and we can see Peter Gabriel's tulip tree. This draws us in to the narrator's world, getting the oxytocin flowing. Then we get that point of stress, in which we feel the narrator's pain: Bezos's grandmother bursting into tears, Cameron's trauma over his desperately ill child, and Gabriel's terrible abuse. This gets the cortisol going. Lastly, the stories resolve with an insight: 'it's harder to be kind than to be clever', 'I value the NHS' and 'we all face common struggles'.

This is how stories work. In a short period of time, we connect with them, feel their pain, share their relief. And we admire their courage in confessing such pain.

The creation of legends

Personal stories make legends out of leaders. Every American child knows the story about George Washington chopping down his father's cherry tree and then confessing to his father: 'I cannot tell a lie, father! I cut it with my little hatchet.' Many business people know about Richard Branson's near-death experience in 1987 when his hot-air balloon almost crashed.

personal stories make legends out of leaders

Stories like these bind us to our leaders. Now, in particular, we live in the age of the confessional. I've seen leaders speak about all sorts of experiences: ranging from abortions and sex attacks right through to the murder of family members. Stuart Rose, the former CEO of Marks and Spencer, has spoken publicly about how awful it was for him when his mother committed suicide. Barack Obama has spoken about how tough he found his teenage years, with a white mother and an absent black father.[1] He was struggling with his identity.

Personal stories like these are unforgettable. These are the moments of truth when people feel connected to the real, unvarnished, authentic leader. The leader shows their vulnerability and this makes it possible to identify with them. When I first became a speechwriter, I used to get frustrated if one of my clients departed from the text to tell a personal story. Now, I am in no doubt: the personal stories are the best bits.

If you want to see storytelling at its best, watch Steve Jobs's amazing Stanford Commencement Address: https://www.youtube.com/watch?v=UF8uR6Z6KLc. He basically tells the story of his whole life in three movements: about being given up for adoption as a baby, about the humiliation of being fired from Apple and being told he had less than six months to live. It's birth, life and death, and concludes with a slogan to die for: 'stay hungry, stay foolish'. Making points through story is much more effective than through simple assertion or through metaphorically thumping people on the head with a 136-page PowerPoint deck.

So, for instance, if you want to get people focused, why not tell them about a time when great focus helped you achieve something magnificent – running a marathon, writing a song, building a house. Or, if you have to convince people about the importance of corporate values, why not tell them a story about your personal values. Was there a moment in your life when you realised that there was more to life than money? I've seen leaders talking about how the most terrible near-death experiences, leaving audiences enthralled.

Stories like this create a deep emotional reaction. That emotional reaction lives forever in people's minds. Neurologists say that once neurons fire together, they wire together.[2] It's known as Hebbian learning: connecting things together simply by talking about them together. So tell stories to make points. People will never forget your stories. And neither will they forget the point you made.

Once neurons fire together, they wire together

What's your story?

Every leader should have their own leadership storybook. But how do you find your own stories? Asking someone to tell a story is a bit like the photographer who sticks a lens in your face and says '*Relax!*' Instead of making people relax, it causes them to freeze. So, if the thought of sharing stories makes you freeze, here's a simple three-point process to thaw you out.

Every leader should have their own leadership storybook

First, get a piece of paper and draw a graph of your life. Chart out the ups and downs as if your life were a share price. Have a time line as the x-axis and a good-to-bad scale as the y-axis. Now put brief notes alongside the peaks and troughs to show what happened, such as 'Elise was born', 'broke leg', 'mum and dad divorced'.

What do these events teach you about yourself and the world? Are there any patterns? You may, for instance, find that moments of tribulation always precede moments of triumph. You may find that major crises regularly provide the impetus for change. Or you might find that the good times and the bad times often run in parallel. For instance, having a baby can be the most joyful time of life but it can also be the toughest.

Then, step two, separately, scribble down on Post-it notes your ten big philosophies for life, the things that matter most to you in the world. Without
wishing to get too morbid, a good way to approach this might be to think,
'If I only had a few moments left to live, what would be the one message
I would want to pass on to my heirs?' I recently spent a day with songwriter
Ian Dench, writing a song for my daughters. The pressure to get the message right was intense. He kept probing me, repeatedly asking, 'But what
do you *really* mean?' In the end, the idea we came up with was, 'in every
day, in every way, you're making your legacy'. That was my message to my
daughers, but what would your message be? See if you can come up with
ten of your personal philosophies for life (e.g. 'give your best', 'treat others
as you would wish to be treated yourself', 'don't give up on your dreams').

Now, step three, join together steps one and two. Match your personal
big-life events to your top-ten philosophies. Stick the Post-it notes of
your philosophies beside the defining moments in your life that you think
might have influenced them. Did the experience of seeing your mum and
dad divorce draw out from you a deep sense of responsibility? Why? What
happened? Take me back there – put me in your shoes. Show me what you
saw. Tell me how it resolved. Perhaps the birth of your first child showed
you the meaning of compassion? Take me back to when it happened. Put
me in your shoes. Tell me what you saw. Tell me how it resolved. What
happened when you looked your son in the eye for the first time?

These are your stories. No one else owns these stories. Keep going, until
you have stories to illustrate each of your ten philosophies. When you
are done, you should have your own leadership storybook in your hand.
Within that storybook lies powerful clues to who you are, where you
come from and why you do what you do. That book contains everything
you need to connect with people emotionally: to raise goose pimples
on their skin, put tears in their eyes and tug on their heartstrings. Keep
that book closed if you want to, but when you finally open it up, you will
realise you are holding in your hands an awesome power.

You will see instantly the different effect you can have upon people. As
soon as a personal story begins, people look up expectantly, the mood

changes: you'll see people willing you on. Your stories will help people feel better about themselves but they will also make you feel better. Research has shown how cathartic it is to tell our own stories.[3] Don't be afraid to go right back: often the most powerful stories come from early on in our lives.[4] It is during our childhood that the narrative develops that shapes our whole lives.

One of the most enjoyable elements of my job is helping other people to tell their stories. On my Language of Leadership workshops, I sometimes ask people to tell me a story that illustrates why a particular philosophy matters to them. On one occasion, I asked for a story to illustrate why hard work matters: a young woman, Teresa Kotlicka, stood up and said this:

> I grew up in a low-income immigrant family in New Jersey. We didn't have much money but my big break came in 1996 when a charity NGO, NJ Seeds, took me on and backed me through secondary school. It changed my life and, for this reason, I was often seen and heard at their fundraising activities and donor events, helping the cause. In the senior year of high school, sitting on my bedroom floor with college financial aid brochures spread around me, I received a phone call from the wife of a prominent executive in financial services. She and her husband wished to donate to NJ Seeds but also, she said that they wanted personally to sponsor my own college education. Without realising the impact then, it meant I would benefit from minimal loans and a chance to study abroad in the South of France. It also meant I wasn't behind my peers in any form, when I arrived on campus to find a computer in my dorm and a prepaid bill at the university bookshop. The couple asked for only one thing in return for their donation: a promise that when I got to a similar position to them in life, I would do the same for someone else. It's a promise I will keep.

She told the story with the authenticity that only comes from first-hand testimony. Her voice cracked at points and occasionally her breath quickened. And, when she finished, there was not a dry eye in the room. As she shared her story, we'd been in her shoes. We'd seen the world from her

eyes. We'd seen those magazines lying around on the floor. We'd picked up the phone with her. That is the Language of Leadership and I tell you, this young woman is not yet 30, but she is well on the way to honouring the commitment she made way back when she was just 13.

What stories would you put in your leadership storybook?

chapter 12

Creating Cultures

'After nourishment, shelter and companionship, stories are the things we need most in the world.'

Philip Pullman

Every family has a collection of stories they love telling and retelling, over and over. These stories might be happy, they might be sad. You know the kind of thing: the stories told after a few drinks at Christmas: stories of miscreant uncles, shock bereavements and hilarious mishaps. These stories bind the family together.

It is stories like these that make a culture. Cultures are little more than collections of stories. Think about any groups you're involved with: football clubs, political parties, social groups, book clubs, circles of friends and so on. It is through the stories of the group that you learn about the values, history and philosophies of that group: where they come from, what they stand for, where they would like to be. Take a country like the United Kingdom.

Cultures are little more than collections of stories

We have stories we constantly tell: about Henry VIII and his wives, the Second World War and Churchill's resistance, the last-minute glory of England's World Cup win in 1966. Don't these stories say something about British spirit?

It falls to the leader to shape and share these stories. By sharing stories, they are shaping the culture. Howard Schultz, CEO of Starbucks, says he spends half his time listening to people telling stories and the other half sharing those stories. He is proactively leading change, exactly as a good leader should.

A leader who does not proactively spread stories may find negative stories rise up in their place. You know the kind of thing: lazy workers who should have been sacked years ago if only management had the courage to tackle them. Stories of millions wasted on failed IT projects. Stories about excessive lunch claims by members of the leadership team. If stories like these are allowed to prevail, an organisation can very quickly slide into decline, with bad behaviours multiplying. The responsible leader creates strong stories to snuff out the negative ones. So where do we find those stories?

Start in the past and work towards the present.

Foundation stories

The first story is about origins. How did the organisation come into being? That story often clearly sets out culture, values and purpose.

Innocent Drinks is a prime example. You might already know their story. Three young university friends went to a music festival in south-west London and set up a stall to sell fruit smoothies. They put a board at the front of their stall asking, 'Do you think we should give up our jobs to sell these full-time?' They had 'yes' and 'no' bins where customers could put their empty bottles. At the end of the day, there were only three bottles in the 'no' bin whilst the 'yes' bin was spilling over.

YouTube's story also has three young founders. They were at a dinner party one night in San Francisco, where they created a load of funny videos but had no means to share them together afterwards. So they came up with the idea of a video-sharing website. The rest is history.[1]

There are plenty of other examples. James Dyson – who grew so frustrated with the poor performance of his vacuum cleaner that he took it apart and rebuilt it, going through hundreds of prototypes before he found one that performed to his high standards. Or Unilever – founded in Victorian Britain – as a philanthropic mission to sell soap in order to tackle poor hygiene in the dirty, overcrowded metropolises of Victorian times.

Every organisation has its own founding stories: from the BBC, the NHS and the Open University to Diabetes UK, Cancer Research and the NSPCC, through to the Conservative, Liberal Democrat and Labour Parties. These stories establish values and beliefs. Great leaders can use these stories to remind people what they are all about: they can use them as carrots to incentivise good behaviour but also as sticks when things go wrong.

For me, one of the most powerful political interventions of recent years in Britain was Theresa May's 2014 speech at the Police Federation, where she castigated the police for a whole series of failings – from Stephen Lawrence to Hillsborough to Iain Tomlinson. She reminded them that Sir Robert Peel had founded the police 200 years previously on the principle of policing by consent. She quoted Peel: 'The Police are the public and the public are the police.' She went on to say that they had betrayed that principle. It was a body blow to those present. Some afterwards said it was the most violent assault they'd ever witnessed (gross hyperbole...). But Theresa May did the job. Good for her.

TABLE 12.1 Appealing to the Declaration of Independence

Lincoln – The Gettysburg Address	'Four score and seven years ago our fathers brought forth on this continent a new nation, conceived in Liberty, and dedicated to the proposition that all men are created equal.'
Martin Luther King – 'I Have a Dream'	'Five score years ago, a great American, in whose symbolic shadow we stand signed the Emancipation Proclamation. This momentous decree came as a great beacon light of hope to millions of Negro slaves who had been seared in the flames of withering injustice. It came as a joyous daybreak to end the long night of captivity. But 100 years later, we must face the tragic fact that the Negro is still not free.'
Barack Obama – 'Yes We Can'	'Tonight, more than 200 years after a former colony won the right to determine its own destiny, the task of perfecting our union moves forward.'

Appeals like these work well within organisations but they also work well at a national level. A country's history has a deep resonance. Many of the most powerful speeches in America's history have harked back to the Declaration of Independence, as shown in Table 12.1.

Case studies

Great leaders will also use case studies: stories that demonstrate the great things that are going on right now, bringing it bang up to date. These stories can be used to present particular messages – our customers come first, it's all about new ways of working. These stories can be used to change behaviour.

Greg Dyke successfully used stories to change culture when he was director-general of the BBC. During the early days of his leadership, three big stories reverberated around the whole organisation, signalling a major shift in approach. First: the nine o'clock news was shifted to ten o'clock. This was the kind of decision that the BBC would, in the past, have agonised over for months – under Dyke, the whole thing went from proposal to execution in less than two weeks. It was brave, it attracted criticism, but it was done. Boom! Second: for many years, the big atrium in the middle of White City Television Centre had been closed for health and safety reasons: people were afraid someone might drown in the two inches of water in the fountains, or some such. But Greg Dyke got the lawyers in, said they were being too risk averse, overruled them and reopened the atrium. This meant that everyone who worked at the BBC could enjoy the atrium and see it bustling with people at lunchtime. Third: he started replying to emails personally from anyone in the corporation – and anyone who received one of these personal emails from Greg went around and told at least 50 people about it.

These stories spread around the BBC like wildfire. They clearly sent a message that the BBC was now a place where people could challenge and take risks. People loved them. And they loved Greg Dyke as well: so much so that when he was forced out of his job, hundreds of BBC employees lined the street to say goodbye to him, many in tears.

Dyke used stories to bring about change. During any change programme, the stories that circulate are crucial. But they must circulate organically: if they are spread by the internal communications team, people will instantly discount and discredit them as 'spin'. You want people to swap these stories themselves. Lead by example. 'Go walkabout' and share what you see. You might discover all sorts of things. Share your stories and tell them in such a way that people really care. At times of change, there is no better antidote to toxic cynicism than first-hand authentic stories.

There is no better antidote to toxic cynicism than first-hand authentic stories

chapter 13

Harnessing History

'History doesn't repeat itself, but it does rhyme.'

Mark Twain

Do you remember Sainsbury's Christmas advert in 2014? They re-created the legendary scene from the trenches in the First World War when British and German soldiers abandoned hostilities for an evening, swapped presents and played football. The evocative advert went viral instantly, appearing on Facebook and Twitter with comments such as 'Oh my God – this made me cry'. The story created a powerful sense of nostalgia and togetherness: moods that then became intertwined with Sainsbury's at Christmas.

History is filled with deeply emotional and evocative stories: stories that touch us deep inside, reminding us of our common humanity – our common hopes and fears. Vietnam. Live Aid. A man on the moon. Tiananmen Square. The fall of the Berlin Wall. These mega-events hit us like thumps in the chest. They are points of universal resonance. But we can go back even further: to Caesar's fall, the Magna Carta or the discovery of America. These are equally

History is filled with deeply emotional and evocative stories

resonant moments. Great leaders use stories like these in support of their argument – and its effect can be awesome.

Even the briefest of references can prove incredibly powerful. The famous picture of the young Vietnamese girl, running naked, scorched by napalm can induce a powerful feeling of shame. A quick glance of the man in Tiananmen Square, standing in front of a tank, can induce pride. A quick glance of Gandhi, being carried away in his blood-soaked clothes, can induce a wave of grief.

Our references don't have to be traumatic: they can be more celebratory. Pelé scoring a goal. The Beatles getting their first number one. Einstein discovering the theory of relativity. Different people draw stories from different places. Their choice of stories sends signs about who they are. But great leaders can use stories from history to sweep people off their feet, picking them up and transporting them somewhere new (Figure 13.1).

FIGURE 13.1 / The gale force of history

Moulding history

Churchill said that history would be kind to him because he intended to write it. Leaders do get an opportunity to rewrite history. And they rewrite history to create a favourable backdrop for their own leadership. George W. Bush told the story of a country built from raw strength and courage, because he presided at a time of fear. Barack Obama told the story of an America in which anything was possible because he wanted to promote unity. History is subjective, not objective: it can prove anything the storyteller wants.

History is subjective, not objective: it can prove anything

Barack Obama's message to the American people was famously 'Yes we can'. As shown in Table 13.1, it would have been equally possible, however, to take another perspective which said 'No we can't'.

TABLE 13.1   Yes we can, or no we can't?

Yes we can (from Obama's victory speech in Chicago, 2008)	No we can't (by Simon Lancaster)
This election had many firsts and many stories that will be told for generations. But one that's on my mind tonight is about a woman who cast her ballot in Atlanta. She's a lot like the millions of others who stood in line to make their voice heard in this election except for one thing - Ann Nixon Cooper is 106 years old.	This election had many firsts and many stories that will be told for generations. But one that's on my mind tonight is about a man who cast his ballot in Washington. He's a lot like the millions of others who stood in line to make his voice heard in this election except for two things – John Edward Wallace is 58 years old and he is also my driver.
She was born just a generation past slavery; a time when there were no cars on the road or planes in the sky; when someone like her couldn't vote for two reasons – because she was a woman and because of the colour of her skin.	He was born just a generation before Sgt Pepper: a time when there was no internet, no HBO, no Justin Bieber, no Kristen Stewart.
And tonight, I think about all that she's seen throughout her century in America – the heartache and the hope; the struggle and the progress; the times we were told that we can't, and the people who pressed on with that American creed: Yes, we can.	Tonight, I think about him and all that he has seen in his lifetime – the tears and tribulations, the doubt and despair, the laziness and loss – the times we were told we could do anything, and the people responded with that American creed: no we can't.

At a time when women's voices were silenced and their hopes dismissed, she lived to see them stand up and speak out and reach for the ballot. Yes, we can.	At a time when preachers, presidents and presidential candidates were standing up, speaking out and reaching for the ballot, he saw them dismissed, shot down and silenced by bullets. No we can't.
When there was despair in the dust bowl and depression across the land, she saw a nation conquer fear itself with a New Deal, new jobs and a new sense of common purpose. Yes, we can.	When the world looked to us for leadership, he watched as we dropped bombs on Laos, committed massacres in Vietnam and engaged in countless futile missions in the Middle East. No we can't.
When the bombs fell on our harbour and tyranny threatened the world, she was there to witness a generation rise to greatness and a democracy was saved. Yes, we can.	When we proclaimed to the world the power of our democracy, he watched as offices were burgled, arms were illegally sold and presidents were impeached. No we can't.
She was there for the buses in Montgomery, the hoses in Birmingham, a bridge in Selma, and a preacher from Atlanta who told a people that 'we shall overcome'. Yes, we can.	He was there for the riots in Los Angeles, the shootings in Columbine and the lawyer who told the jury, 'if the glove don't fit, you must acquit'. No we can't.
A man touched down on the Moon, a wall came down in Berlin, a world was connected by our own science and imagination. And this year, in this election, she touched her finger to a screen, and cast her vote, because after 106 years in America, through the best of times and the darkest of hours, she knows how America can change. Yes, we can.	A rock star died on the toilet. A film star put a bullet through his own head. Any sense of global unity fell to one side. And this year in this election, he touched his finger to a screen and cast his vote, because after 58 years in America, through the best of times and the darkest of hours, he knows that America can't change. No we can't.

Topicality

Leaders can also mould topical events to make points. It depends what's going on: the final of *The X Factor*, a big film being released, a royal baby being born, a sporting event, a historic anniversary… All have the potential to sweep people along.

Personally, I found it very inspiring in 2012 when Felix Baumgartner sky dived from a hot-air balloon 24 miles up in the sky, free-falling from space at over 800 miles an hour. This was fairly big news when it happened. I watched it with my daughter Lottie on my lap: we were both transfixed

TABLE 13.2   A skydive: for or against regulation?

The Case for Regulation	The Case against Regulation
Anyone see that amazing skydive last weekend? Wasn't it incredible? When I first saw it, I thought, he must be crazy. But when I saw him interviewed I realized he wasn't crazy: his dive had been meticulously prepared every step of the way. He spent years in training, working with the best. As the date of the jump got closer, he was continually revisiting and revising his plans. On the original date, he cancelled the skydive, because the weather was not right. As he was going up in the balloon, he realized that his visor was steaming up – but he decided to continue in any case, because he knew the ground control team could keep him in touch. Then, during his descent, he started spinning uncontrollably. He knew that he could stop spinning by arching his back but he feared that doing that would foil his record-breaking attempt. So instead of being reckless, what he was doing, at every step of the way, was carefully measuring, managing and mitigating against risks. That is exactly what we have to do in setting regulation…	Anyone see the amazing skydive last weekend? Wasn't it amazing? Isn't it amazing what human beings can achieve when they put their minds to something? It's the same drive that led people to discover penicillin, to invent the jet engine, to develop the worldwide web. The human spirit will grapple with any problem that is thrown at it. At the moment, we are grappling with some serious problems. Climate change. Terrorism. The worst financial crisis in 70 years. The worst thing to do now would be to put shackles on people's freedom. This could prevent us finding the proper path out from this crisis. We need not more regulation, but less…

(oxytocin and cortisol, obviously). If you want to get the oxytocin and cortisol flowing, just showing that video will do the trick. But you can use that story to prove your point, whatever your point happens to be. In fact, it is no stretch to say that I believe, with careful positioning, you can use almost any story to prove almost any point. Table 13.2 illustrates how the skydive story can be used to make the case both in defence of regulation and against regulation.

Mythological stories

If you don't want to use a historic or topical story, you can always use a fable. Certain fables gather particular currency at particular times. In 2015 it seems fashionable to make the 'burning platform' speech. You might have heard this. There is a man who is working on an oil platform. He discovers the platform has caught fire. He climbs to the edge. He is faced with a terrifying choice. What does he do? Stand and wait to be consumed by the flames? Or jump into the freezing waters and swim for his life?

This is a great story in two respects. When it is told, people identify with the protagonist, getting the oxytocin flowing. They also feel the cortisol going when the dilemma is described. However, it lacks the third essential step. The resolution. The dopamine.

Stephen Elop told the burning platform story to Nokia staff when he became CEO. I had friends who worked for Nokia at the time. I heard that it split the company in two: some thought this message was necessary; others thought it was over the top, too far.

The trouble with the burning platform story for me is that it offers great stress without resolution. Stressing people out is not a great way to achieve change. When people have cortisol flowing in their brains all their focus is on getting rid of the threat. They cannot think of anything else. This makes change, innovation and transformation impossible. If you really want to foster change, a better strategy is to make people feel good about themselves. Instead of cortisol, we want serotonin, oxytocin and dopamine. This is where appeals to values can prove so effective, which takes us on to the next chapter in the Language of Leadership.

chapter 14

The Value of Values

'A system of morality which is based on relative emotional values is a mere illusion, a thoroughly vulgar conception which has nothing sound in it and nothing true.'

Socrates

Values are – as the word suggests – the things in life that we most value. Whilst our opinions blow with the wind and our attitudes change over time, our values and beliefs tend to remain fixed throughout our lives.

Everyone has different values and everyone's values are unique. Our values are shaped by our own unique collection of experiences such as our education, our upbringing and our religion (if we have any). Our values act as our spiritual GPS. They tell us which way to go. They determine how we think, feel and act.

Everyone's values are unique

Great leaders know how to harness these values. They use values to lead: to make people care about what they do, to focus more sharply and work harder. You might run a bus company. The bus drivers might see their job as depressing. A good leader would remind them about the power of human connection (the values statement). A simple smile. A small gesture. The touch of a hand. They might point out that, for the old lady getting on the bus in the morning, the bus driver might be her only point of contact throughout the course of the day. A simple event such as whether or not the bus driver greets her with a smile or not could make all the difference between her having a bad day or a good day… By invoking values you can engage, excite and inspire.

Great leaders recognise that different people have different values and judge their appeals accordingly. Someone who grew up in a small village community with regular litter-picking sessions, harvest festivals and social events might have a profound belief in what people can achieve by working together. Someone who was subjected to cruelty or abuse during their childhood may believe that if you want something done well, you should do it yourself: you can't rely on anyone else. The great leader will recognise these different backgrounds and try to get the best out of each of them by making appeals based on their own unique values.

Great leaders often connect values to a company's core purpose, which we covered between pages 80 and 87. This is a potent mix: research shows that businesses built on a higher purpose and values outperform the market by ten to one.[1] Table 14.1 shows some examples of how great leaders connect purpose to values. The million-dollar prize comes from connecting day-to-day tasks to these strategic purposes and deepest values.

Businesses built on a higher purpose and values outperform the market by ten to one

TABLE 14.1   Connecting corporate purpose and values

Leader	Purpose	Value
Henry Ford, Ford	Democratising the automobile: putting a car in the reach of every man and woman who earns a good salary.	Hard work should be rewarded.
Bob Shapiro, Monsanto	Tackling global hunger.	Everyone on the planet should be fed.
Laura Bates, Everyday Sexism	Creating equality.	People should be treated fairly.

When values collide

Anchoring in values is relatively straightforward. I wrote extensively about this in *Speechwriting: The Expert Guide*. But what happens when values collide? This is an increasingly common dilemma. You might get someone who is fastidious about cleanliness in their personal life, but who works for a company that produces a lot of pollution. You might get someone who, in their personal life, always buys Fairtrade products, but who works for a company that treats its suppliers shabbily. You might get someone who, in their personal life, behaves with utter responsibility but who works for a company which does not mind letting down its customers.

Many people struggle with dilemmas like these. Combined with peer pressure, it can place people in an invidious position where they feel forced to choose between their personal values and professional duties. It is the leader's responsibility to help people navigate their way through these dilemmas. People should not feel there is a clash between their personal and professional lives. Asking someone to shed their personal values when they come to work is like asking them to leave behind a vital part of who they are. This will guarantee that they are unable to give 100%, forcing them to become part performers, leading inevitably, in the jargon, to them becoming 'emotionally disengaged'.

I personally found it very difficult writing speeches in support of the Iraq War. I felt incredibly uncomfortable about the whole thing: the lack of consensus, the disrespect of the United Nations, rich nations attacking poor nations. I felt positively queasy, particularly as I was writing parliamentary speeches arguing in favour of the war. It was my two oldest and closest friends – Mike and Dave – who basically put me in my place: they reminded me that I was not a democratically elected leader, rather it was my job to support democratically elected leaders. Or, as Mike more succinctly put it, 'Who the f*ck do you think you are? Robin Cook or something?' This shift in focus helped me see things another way. Not everyone was able to deal with the values clash: some civil servants walked out over Iraq. It was very difficult – no doubt – but that is why great leaders must always pay regard to people's values. If they don't, they can quickly wind up with major trouble on their hands.

Some organisations have written values. If this is the case, to be effective, they should accurately reflect people's values rather than being something prepared on the back of a fag packet. I once heard about one CEO who went into a new business and announced on his first day, 'Right, here are your new values.' There had been no consultation, no discussion. He put a PowerPoint slide on the screen with just five words on it. These were the values of the last company he'd worked at. He hadn't even taken the trouble to remove his former employer's logo. And the words were the kind that instantly make the heart sink: accountability, frugality, collaboration, diversity and resilience. To touch people emotionally, we must use emotional language. That takes us on to the next secret from the Language of Leadership: words we love.

chapter 15

Great Words We Love

'Words are the most powerful drug used by mankind.'
Rudyard Kipling

The trouble with my line of work is that, when someone gives feedback on a speech, I know what they *really* mean. If someone says 'Exquisite. Beautiful. Great feeling' I know that I have hit the spot. However, if someone says 'Good. Working well. Like the structure', I know I could have done better. There are some words that people only use when their emotions are flowing, and other words that show they are not really bothered.

The thing is: words do not sit in our brains in isolation. Each word is surrounded by its own connotations, memories and associations. Each time we hear that word used, these connotations, memories and associations are invoked.

Now I don't know about you, but every time I've heard the words collaborative, benchmarking, framework, deliverables and beacons it has been in a phenomenally dull context. That means whenever I hear these words now, my brain can't help but switch off, anticipating a long period of dullness. In contrast, there are other words that I've only ever heard at good times: honey, love, champagne, diamonds, chocolate – these are words that have a deep emotional resonance. These words make my ears prick up.

Some words sparkle and sizzle, others fall flat

Where some words sparkle and sizzle, others fall flat. And this affects how people behave.

Harvard University did some fascinating research on a group of older people. They asked them to play a computer game that tested their mental powers. What the older people didn't know was that, whilst they were playing the game, words were flashing up subliminally on the screen. Half of the group were given positive words about being older, such as wise, astute and accomplished; the other half were given more negative words such as senile, dependent and diseased. The group who had received the positive words walked 10% faster when they left.[1] So using words with positive associations can boost performance by 10%.

Using words with positive associations can boost performance by 10%

Great leaders choose their words with care. They find words that support, rather than sabotage, their aims. When appropriate, they find words which will have an emotional resonance. This is not to say that leaders always want to touch people emotionally. Sometimes leaders deliberately want to be boring. Many politicians and business people regard being boring as a vital tactical device. That's fine, as long as that really is their aim. Sometimes leaders actively want to take emotion out of a situation: for instance, during a period of restructuring or redundancies, we might want to use less emotionally fraught language. Terms such as collateral damage and friendly fire serve a similar purpose in war.

But too many leaders are boring by default rather than by design. If you want to praise people, and you want to inspire them to do greater things in future, your words must be emotional. Saying 'Your performance was significantly above requirements' is not going to touch anyone emotionally. It might be better to say something like, 'I loved what you did this year. It was great. Really great.'

So how can we find these emotional words? If we want to be really serious and analytical about it, there are some American professors – James Pennebaker, Roger Booth and Martha Francis – who have developed software that systematically analyses text and groups and scores it according to different emotions (e.g. anger, hope, passion, shame and more). The software is available at www.liwc.net. It's sometimes amazing, sometimes amusing but inherently subjective.

Another way to do it is to try to find your own language. You can use whatever source you like. I've done this in a very quick and easy way, just taking the best quotes from Disney and the biggest songs of The Beatles and making word clouds out of them (by the way, you can create your own word clouds if you want – just paste the text you want into www. wordle.net and a word cloud will be automatically generated). I figure that Disney and The Beatles have a well-proven record when it comes to touching people emotionally. Their word clouds are quite interesting. You can see some recurring words.

First, here is a word cloud of the biggest Beatles songs:

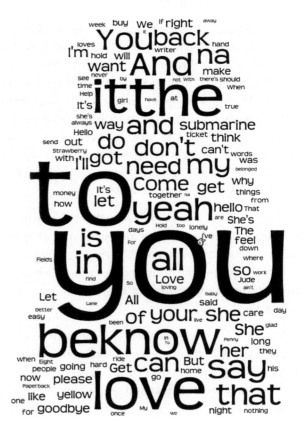

And here is a word cloud of the most memorable lines from Disney's top films:

You can see how the words are similar in each of the two word clouds. The one overleaf, on the other hand, is a word cloud from a fairly typical report about public service change.

Bit different, aren't they? Do a word cloud of some of your biggest documents. Do you think that you are emotional enough for your purpose? Do you think you could use more emotional language?

Cheat list

There are other words that I think of as word bombs: words that can prove explosive, dropped in the right place at the right time. The list in Table 15.1 is not developed scientifically but just based on experience. These are words that, for me, provide a quick shortcut to the emotions. These are the oxytocin and serotonin words, feel-good words: words that crop up over and over again in the Language of Leadership.

There are plenty of other words you could add to those shown in Table 15.1: dream (did Martin Luther say 'I have a global strategy?'), 'believe' (never 'think' always 'believe' – don't be half-hearted, show conviction!), imagine (a word that can instantly transport someone to a better place) and many more. Maybe build up your own little list of your favourite oxytocin and serotonin words.

It is worth emphasising that words can and do go in and out of fashion. Excellence was all the rage in the 1980s – excellence in construction, excellence in HR, excellence in management – then along came *Bill and Ted's Excellent Adventure* and that was it: kaput. Who knows? Maybe one day great will grate.

A word bomb can guarantee that people notice some otherwise bland prose. A leading educational think tank called the Sutton Trust recently published an empirical review of research into pedagogy. It doesn't sound so scintillating like that but they gave it the title: 'What makes great teaching' and – boom! – the report won loads of publicity.

TABLE 15.1   Word bombs

I, Me, You, Your, Us, Our	A great conversation requires people to be present. You need people speaking and listening. The easiest way to achieve that is through use of pronouns such as I, me, mine, you, your, yours, we, our, us and so on. In academic text, pronouns are strangely absent: it makes the writing abnormally distant and impersonal, with no sense of writer or reader. There is a disproportionate use of pronouns in the Language of Leadership. Barack Obama said 'Yes we can', not 'Change is possible'. Steve Jobs branded his smartphones not as advanced mobile phones but as iPhones. Paul McCartney once gave an interview explaining that it was pronouns that made The Beatles' songs so 'very personal'… 'Please Please <u>Me</u>', 'From <u>Me</u> to <u>You</u>', 'PS <u>I</u> Love <u>You</u>', '<u>She</u> Loves <u>You</u>'.
Great	'Great' has always touched deeply – from *Great Expectations* to *The Great Gatsby*; from IBM to Tony the Tiger; from 'Good to Great' to 'Insanely Great'. Great is the kind of word used by family, friends and a kindly teacher. Not good, but great. Great has now supplanted the word 'excellent' as the word to use in business.
Love	Love is the most important thing to all of us when it really comes down to it. And when the word is used, we're thinking of those needs. The word love features all over the place in business and particularly advertising, from 'We're lovin' it' (McDonald's) to 'Love the skin you're in' (Olay) and 'Quality you can love' (Nissan).

Just dropping in the word 'love' elevates a sentence from the functional to the emotional. I recently saw some girls' dresses that were labelled 'made with love in India'. It's a bit nicer than just 'made in India', which could conjure up pictures of sweatshops and so on. Later on, at a friend's house I saw their organic veg box that had apparently been 'packed with love by Emma'. Both products were priced at a premium of 50% over the usual market price. So money can't buy you love but love can win you money. This thought takes us beautifully into the next chapter, about the power of love.

chapter 16

Flattery and Love

'Flattery raises downcast spirits, comforts the sad, rouses the apathetic, stirs up the stolid, cheers the sick, restrains the headstrong, brings lovers together and keeps them united.'

Erasmus

According to the *Guinness Book of Records*, the most successful salesperson in history is a guy from Detroit called Joe Girard. Between 1963 and 1978, Joe Girard sold a whopping 13,001 cars at a Chevrolet dealership, averaging six car sales a day. When asked the secret of his success, he explained, 'People want a fair deal from someone they like.' So how did he get people to like him? 'Simple,' he replied, 'I tell them that I like them.'

Flattery is one of the oldest techniques in the book. Aristotle wrote in *Rhetoric*, 'It's not hard to praise Athenians amongst Athenians.' The first-ever Archbishop of Canterbury's first words on reaching southern England were, 'These are not Angles [i.e. English], but angels!' Machiavelli also wrote a great deal about flattery in *The Prince*, but flattery is not just something practised by the ancients, it is just as effective today. And even though the word flattery has pejorative connotations, it's just about giving people what they need. We all love to be loved, we all love to be celebrated, even when we know that that celebration is not wholly sincere.

A study was carried out in which a shop sent out random mailshots to all its customers. The mailshots were stuffed with phoney praise, completely over the top, saying they were delighted to have 'customers like you' who are so 'fashionable, stylish, classy and chic'.[1] Even though the recipients knew the compliments were insincere, they still felt warmer towards that shop as a result. They were also more likely to spend money in that shop as a result of those compliments. The research paper was called 'Insincere flattery actually works'.

Why flattery works

When people receive praise, serotonin is released in their brain: making them feel proud and confident. Serotonin is the pride drug, the status-symbol drug, the same drug that makes us feel great when we buy a new suit or get loads of likes on Facebook. Serotonin makes people feel great: and it isn't only released in the person being praised, research shows that the person doing the praising also experiences higher serotonin levels. This builds a connection with them, boosting oxytocin levels. And, more still: because people are always on the lookout for praise, great feedback therefore fulfils expectations, activating a beautiful squirt of dopamine.[2]

That's why flattery improves performance, involvement and commitment levels. It makes people feel great. It's the law of reciprocity – the most basic rule in human interaction.[3] If you make people feel great, they will feel bound to give something back. A study showed that paying people compliments can increase the number of people prepared to help by 30%.[4] And the *Compliments can increase the number of people prepared to help by 30%* people who work for you will work harder than ever before.

Creating a supportive environment

So… give a little love. When things go right, look out of the window; when things go wrong, look in the mirror. Reprimand in private, praise in public. Stop focusing on what people are doing wrong, look at what they are doing right. If you find it difficult to see the good, try to remember they are just people, with mothers, fathers and families who love them. As their leader, it is your job to give a little love too.

Don't forget: the burden of pressure falls not at the top of organisations, but at the bottom.[5] The death rate is four times higher at the bottom of the organisation than the top.[6] It's your responsibility to alleviate stress. Low serotonin levels make people aggressive, angry and impulsive. High serotonin levels make people confident, strong and capable. What kind of workforce would you prefer?[7] There are two ways to lift the serotonin levels: Prozac or praise. Which do you think is better?

The bottom line is this: no matter how frustrated you feel, it is self-defeating to admit it. So always look for something, anything, however little, to praise. You can change your own perspective and change your team's performance. Plus it will make you feel better. What is there to lose?

Some people worry about flattery. They worry that their motives will be transparent. Don't worry: most people don't challenge praise. The truth is that most people believe they're better than they really are anyway. Who thinks they are below average at driving or sex? So the chances are that they'll just assume you're being sincere. If you're worried, you can always sneak in a qualifier, such as 'I know you don't want to hear this, but…' Or, you can send your feedback through a third party: telling someone their friend is brilliant is bound to get back to that individual before long.

Flattery is just about paying regard to people's feelings. And if it is a dishonesty, flattery is a noble dishonesty. Honesty is not always the best policy. My six-year-old daughter can be honest to the point of destruction, pointing at people in cafés and saying 'Isn't he fat?' and 'Daddy, is that woman about to die?' It's like Frank Skinner's 'That was the two hundred

Flattery is a noble dishonesty

and forty-fifth best sex I have had in my whole life.' It might be true but some things are just best not said.

Look at Table 16.1: the difference between the brutally honest CEO and the flatterer. Who would you sooner have as your leader?

Convinced yet? If not, maybe you like the way that both of the leaders in Table 16.1 used repetition. Repetition is another way to touch the emotional brain. It's also the next part of the Language of Leadership...

TABLE 16.1   The honest leader vs the flattering leader

The Honest Leader	The Flattering Leader
I hate going through these rituals. Get everyone together. Make us feel united. Blurgh. Let's be straight. This company is not united. There are just 10% of you moving this company forward. The rest of you are just collecting your cheques. You think I don't know you spend your day on Facebook? You think I don't know you take two hours for lunch? You think I don't know that seven of you are drafting books on the work computer? I can't be doing with it...	I am often asked what inspires me on a day-to-day basis. The answer is simple. It is you. It is the pride I feel when I see you at work. It is the passion I feel when I ask you what you're working on. It is the purpose I feel when I look out at you all now. You are the people who make me love my job. You are the people who make me want to give my heart and soul to this company. You are the people who make me leap out of bed in the morning.

chapter 17

Repetition. Repetition. Repetition

> 'People need to be reminded more than they need to be instructed.'
>
> Samuel Johnson

Special advisers in Whitehall are, as the term implies, special. Some are especially charming. Others are especially obnoxious. I'll never forget hearing about one particularly offensive special adviser who said to their Secretary of State shortly after arriving at a new department, 'You can't trust the press office, you can't trust the economists, you can't trust the lawyers...' And so the list went on. You can easily see how this kind of repetition could sweep a new arrival along, instilling in them a sense of fear, creating a powerful emotional reaction. That's what repetition does. It communicates emotion.

Repetition communicates emotion

Repetition occurs naturally in conversation when we care about what we're saying, such as a drunken barstool preacher mouthing off about his ex-wife ('She's taken my house, she's taken my kids, she's even taken the bleedin' dog'). It's wholly natural. An idea becomes fixed in our mind so it becomes fixed in our language. So repetition in speech is a natural manifestation of an emotionally fixated mind.

Great leaders deliberately use repetition. This creates the illusion of authentic, spontaneous emotion even when they are speaking from a pre-prepared text. Perhaps the most famous example of this was Winston Churchill's, 'We shall fight on the beaches, we shall fight on the landing grounds, we shall fight in the fields and in the streets, we shall fight in the hills…' Churchill could have expressed this much more quickly if he had wanted. And, indeed, had the Plain English Campaign visited Downing Street, they would probably have said, 'Now, Winston. You can say this much faster. Why not just say, "We shall fight on the beaches, landing grounds, fields, streets and hills?" removing all this pointless repetition?' But the repetition was not pointless. The repetition relayed his emotion – his determination and courage – and that was the whole point.

Another famous example is Martin Luther King's 'I have a dream' speech:

> I have a dream that one day this nation will rise up and live out the true meaning of its creed: 'We hold these truths to be self-evident: that all men are created equal'. I have a dream that one day on the red hills of Georgia the sons of former slaves and the sons of former slave owners will be able to sit down together at the table of brotherhood. I have a dream that one day even the state of Mississippi, a state sweltering with the heat of injustice, sweltering with the heat of oppression, will be transformed into an oasis of freedom and justice. I have a dream that my four little children will one day live in a nation where they will not be judged by the color of their skin, but by the content of their character. I have a dream today.

Management consultants would almost certainly have omitted the repetition and just put the essential elements of King's dream as bullet points on a PowerPoint slide.

Malala Yousafzai, one of the most influential young leaders in the world today, said in her famous speech to the United Nations:

> I speak not for myself but for those without voice. Those who have fought for their rights. Their right to live in peace. Their right to be treated with dignity. Their right to equality of opportunity. Their right to be educated.

Repetition works in a number of ways. People recognise the passion – every repetition feels like a silent thump on the table. They predict the pattern, activating a reward cycle of dopamine when their expectations are fulfilled. They are also more likely to be won over as the argument becomes familiar. Research shows that people are more likely to believe a statement is true if they have heard it before, regardless of whether or not it is true.[1]

People are more likely to believe a statement is true if they've heard it before

Repetition can be used in many different ways. Sometimes, slogans will be repeated: Barack Obama repeated 'Yes we can' constantly in broadcasts, speeches, interviews and appearances over a period of two years. Sometimes it can be repetition of just a couple of words such as 'That was wrong – so wrong', providing a rhetorical underlining. This is what Neil Kinnock did in his 1985 speech to the Labour Party conference when he attacked the 'grotesque chaos' of councillors scuttling around in taxis to hand out redundancy notices from 'a Labour council – a *Labour* council'.

Some people like to repeat individual words over and over, a bit like a hypnotist, gently impregnating the subconscious. Gordon Brown spoke in this manner: a word cloud of a Brown speech typically shows just five or six words in disproportionate use to every other word. His general pattern was to repeat a single word once every sentence or so for about ten sentences and then move on to another word. He used this technique in a major speech he made shortly before the referendum on Scottish independence – a speech that some said tipped the balance in favour of the union. The speech was massively emotional so repetition, appropriately, featured throughout.

He used the word 'proud' eight times in the first 120 words: 'We are *proud* of our Scottish identity, *proud* of our distinctive Scottish institutions, *proud* of the Scottish Parliament that we, not the Nationalist Party, created...'

He then used the words 'we' and 'together' repeatedly: 'And we not only won these wars together, we built the peace together, we built the health service together, we built the welfare state together, we will build the future together…'

Then, there was repetition around the words 'their' and 'everyone': 'And let us tell the nationalists this is not their flag, their country, their culture, their streets. This is everyone's flag, everyone's country, everyone's culture and everyone's street…'

Then, the word 'risk' took centre-stage: 'Real risk one: the uncertainty about the currency, unaddressed by the SNP. Real risk two: the default from debt that they threaten, unaddressed by the SNP. Real risk three: having to build £30 billion of reserves at the cost of the NHS and the welfare state…'

Finally, he landed on the word 'confidence': 'Have confidence, have confidence tomorrow and have confidence enough to say with all our friends: we've had no answers. They [the SNP] do not know what they are doing. They are leading us into a trap. Have confidence and say to our friends: for reasons of solidarity, sharing, justice, pride in Scotland, the only answer for Scotland's sake and for Scotland's future is vote "No".'

Many commentators said that it was a great speech. In my opinion, it carried all the hallmarks of vintage Brown: it was typically repetitive, angry and defensive, but, for once, this was the kind of speech that people wanted. This manner hadn't worked so well when he was speaking about local enterprise partnerships, but cometh the moment, cometh the man.

Concerns about using repetition

I never cease to be amazed at the power of repetition. On the page it can look a bit silly – a bit like a children's novel – which turns some people off. The advisers to both Martin Luther King and Winston Churchill repeatedly urged them to cut out the repetition from their speeches, but I never cease to be amazed by its power to sweep people up and leave them high. With repetition, no one can ignore your message.

Repetition can be used in all sorts of scenarios, from market stalls ('I'm not asking £20, I'm not asking £15, I'm not even asking £10...') to inspirational speeches ('We're great at service, we're great at coming up with new ideas, we're great at making big things happen...') to investment seminars ('The fund went up in 2012, the fund went up in 2013, the fund went up in 2014...').

People will usually keep nodding along with repetition, provided you don't say something completely downright insensitive, as happened once when Jimmy Carter was making a speech to an audience of feminists and he said:

> 'The American people believe in justice.' ('Yeah!')
>
> 'The American people believe in fairness.' ('Yeah!')
>
> 'The American people believe in brotherhood.' ('Boooooo....!')

Repetition is the linguistic expression of emotional fixation. Another linguistic expression of emotional fixation is exaggeration: this takes us on to our next and final chapter in winning over the emotional mind...

The Eternal Power of Exaggeration

chapter 18

'Man exaggerates everything… except his own mistakes.'
Unknown

Have you ever found yourself up late at night, worrying about something seriously trivial? Did you reply to that email? Did you unplug the iron? Did you put the chain on the door? No matter what you try, you just can't shake it out of your head.

When we are emotional, our perspective becomes distorted. We can't help it. It is wholly natural. And although distorted perspective is a trait often associated with immaturity or childishness, anthropologists actually think that the development of our capacity to distort perspective represented a critical step in our evolution.

You can see the precise point in history when the Broca's area of the brain started to enlarge. There were dramatic changes in cave art. All of a sudden, artists started to deliberately distort scale to convey emotion. So fierce animals were painted with disproportionate horns, tusks and teeth to communicate danger. Paintings of women started to feature disproportionately large breasts and genitalia to communicate rewards…[1] Distorting perspective became an exciting new element in communication. It meant we could convey messages more powerfully than ever before. It gave us a better chance of communicating information that could prove crucial to the survival of the human race.

Distorted perspective is also an essential element in the Language of Leadership. The ancient Greeks had a term for it: hyperbole. Hyperbole is often cast in a negative light but it is a technique that generations of religious leaders, monarchs, emperors, business leaders and scientific gurus have relied upon to make their points successfully. Just look back through history books and speech anthologies: leaders have always exaggerated – presenting the world as perpetually either on the brink of utopia or the edge of the Apocalypse; had they presented a more honest 'life goes on' message, they would never have been able to lead the change they wanted. Straightforward logic does not have the same power to sweep people off their feet. We move people through emotion. Exaggeration is emotion.

People naturally exaggerate to communicate their emotional state, from self-loathing ('I can't get anything right these days'), to envy ('he's a total nightmare'), to pride ('I blew his socks off!'), to sorrow ('my dad's always working'), to passion ('it was the most amazing night ever'), to fear ('he's a pyscho!'), to excitement ('it's the job of my dreams'), to hunger ('I could eat a horse'). All of us do it all the time. I get so excited about exaggeration. I could talk about it forever.

Exaggeration works

Great leaders tend to exaggerate more than most. That is because they are visionaries. They have exciting visions which carry them away and take over their minds. It is only because their own minds are so dominated that they are able to dominate the minds of others: this is how they create change: sweeping people away, steamrolling logic, transforming the world from the world it is to the world they want. Emotion trumps reason. As George Bernard Shaw once wrote: 'The reasonable man adapts himself to the world; the unreasonable one persists in trying to adapt the world to himself. Therefore all progress depends on the unreasonable man.'

Exaggeration excites: it gets the endorphins flowing. Just think of history's great leaders. They all exaggerated. Churchill, Jobs, Thatcher, Hitler, Stalin, Bin Laden. These were not straight talkers. They used exaggeration to draw people in, make them care and move them. And exaggeration changes people's view of the world.

Exaggeration excites: it gets the endorphins flowing

The media regularly exaggerates to make its points and this seriously affects people's outlooks. MORI research shows that people think that benefit fraud is 34 times higher than it is, that teenage pregnancy is 25 times higher than it is and that immigration is three times higher than it is. Such distortions change the political debate and govern the way people vote.[2]

Practical application

Exaggeration is not necessarily a bad thing. Sometimes people actively want to be swept along and made to feel better about what they do: so exaggeration can be a good way of meeting people's emotional needs. There might be a political group that is feeling a little jaded, a workforce which feels disillusioned and dispirited, a charity that is struggling to see the light at the end of the tunnel. The exaggeration may be deceptive but, as with flattery, it is a noble deception – saying things like 'This is a once-in-a-lifetime opportunity', 'It doesn't get better than this' or 'I'm giving my heart and soul to this company' is not going to hurt anyone.

Exaggeration is obviously not always appropriate. If you are addressing a group of the more sceptical – such as lawyers, journalists, speechwriters – you should be on your guard, or, at least qualify any exaggerative statements with a 'don't you think?' or 'wouldn't you say?' That's what I always do anyway. There's nothing at all wrong with it, don't you think?

Enough ideas for how to win over the emotional mind? Ready to move on? Come on then. Let's go up another level and take a look at the logical mind.

Part III
Winning the Logical Mind

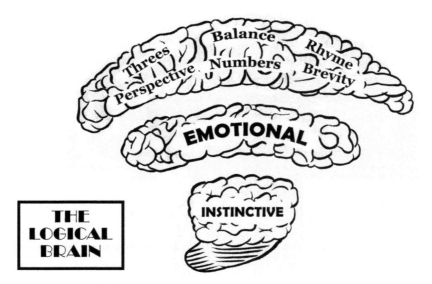

FIGURE PT III.1 / The logical brain

'People are masterful spin-doctors, rationalisers and justi-
fiers of threatening information and go to great lengths to
maintain a sense of well-being.'

Timothy D. Wilson

The logical mind?

Everyone likes to believe they are supremely logical, with brains like super-fast computers, instantly processing complex information and using that to generate hyper-accurate conclusions. But it doesn't work like that. The reality is that, for most people, life is too busy to indulge in the luxury of logic.

Even when people swear they are being rational, fMRI shows they are not. Neuroscientists have shown time and again how little we use our analytical faculties. When we are surfing the web, our brains are effectively on auto pilot. When we are attending university lectures, our brain activity levels are actually lower than when we are asleep.[1] When people are receiving what they believe to be expert advice, the part of the brain that generates alternatives actually shuts down.

People are not as logical as we might hope. What most people do, instead of scrutinising and analysing logic to check that something is right, is look for patterns that suggest something is right. So, if you've done the work set out in the previous chapters, establishing trust and creating a sweep of emotion, you're already most of the way there. But creating the *appearance* of logic is the icing on the cake. We do that through creating pleasing and predictable patterns in the sound and structure of our arguments.

Sequencing arguments

Everyone loves patterns. This is why we love quiz shows, crosswords and sudoku puzzles. We try to find patterns, even when none exist. You know the kind of thing. 'First, we were told we needed a new roof. Then the car packed up. Now, I'm just waiting for the third thing to happen.' When we identify a pattern occurring, we feel a sense of pleasure – a feeling of order in a chaotic world.

Great leaders play into this love of patterns in the way they sequence their arguments. They present their views in ready-made patterns to bolster the illusion of logic. They do so because, in the Language of Leadership, it's not simply the substance of an argument that matters, but also the sound.

It's not simply the substance of an argument that matters, it's the sound

Matching sound and substance

Neuroscientists have shown that there are two separate parts of the brain that process what people say: the left brain processes the meaning whilst the right brain processes the music.[2] Great leaders win over both parts of the brain at once. They do this using ancient 'rhetorical devices' – ways of structuring sentences.

I mentioned rhetorical devices briefly in Chapter 1. In ancient Greece everyone used to learn rhetorical devices at school. Rhetoric has since slipped off the curriculum but the same devices remain just as powerful as ever. And, not only that, they work right around the world, from the West to

FIGURE PT III.2 / **The meaning and the music**

the Middle East, Latin America to the Far East. So these devices cannot be cultural, they must be biologically rooted – based upon how the human brain works. We can speculate as to why this might be but the bottom line is this: it works. Great leaders under- stand the power of rhetorical devices: Boris Johnson recently wrote about Churchill: 'the music of the speech [matters] more than the logic or the substance. It's the sizzle, not the sausage.'

Great leaders know the power of rhetorical devices

Rhetorical devices are not just confined to the spoken word. They are just as powerful in written text. Read these opening lines of *Lolita* by Vladimir Nabokov:

> Lolita, light of my life, fire of my loins. My sin, my soul. Lo-lee-ta: the tip of the tongue taking a trip of three steps down the palate to tap, at three, on the teeth. Lo. Lee. Ta.

Hear it? Thought so. That's because our brains developed primarily to deal with the spoken word. Writing is a relatively recent innovation, dating back only about 4500 years or so. Our brains haven't really changed since then, so sound is still the basis of communication, not sight.

Incidentally, that beautiful little snippet from *Lolita* uses every single one of the devices we examine in Part III: the rule of three, balance, allitera- tion, perspective, numbers and brevitas. These techniques are all secrets of the Language of Leadership and they are all ways to win over the logical mind. Using these devices will make your arguments not just plausible, but palatable. You'll be amazed at the difference they make. Let's start with one of the easiest of all: the 'rule of three'.

19

Threes! Threes! Threes!

'*Omne trium perfectum*'.

Ancient Roman saying

Steve Jobs, Steve Jobs, Steve Jobs

When Steve Jobs launched the iPhone in 2008, he had everything to lose. His move into the crowded mobile-phone market was audacious, even by his standards. He spent months working on his product launch and his script went through several edits and redrafts. The irony was that, for all the cutting-edge technology in the iPhone, the text in his product launch was based around a rhetorical device that had existed for thousands of years.

Check this out:

Steve Jobs – the iPhone launch

This is a day I've been looking forward to for two and a half years. Every once in a while, a revolutionary product comes along that changes everything. Apple's been very fortunate to introduce a few of these into the world.

In 1984, we introduced the Macintosh. It didn't just change Apple, it changed the whole computer industry. In 2001, we introduced the first iPod. And it didn't just change the way we listen to music, it changed the entire music industry. Well, today we're introducing three revolutionary products of this class.

The first is a widescreen iPod with touch controls. The second is a revolutionary mobile phone. And the third is a breakthrough internet communications device. So three things. Are you getting it? These are not three separate devices, this is one device.

But before we get to it, let me talk about 'smart phones', so they say. And they typically combine a phone, plus some email capability and the baby internet. But the trouble is they're not so smart and they're not so easy to use.

So we're going to reinvent the phone.

See how he bundles everything in threes? The history of Apple is crunched into three, even though anyone who knows anything about Apple knows it was far more convoluted than that. The iPhone's features are also boiled down to three – internet explorer, touch-screen iPod and the revolutionary mobile phone – what of the revolutionary camera, a mobile library and gamer? Even when he was attacking the competition – the 'so-called smart-phones' – he still got it down to three: phone, email capability and the baby internet.

But Jobs did the job. The iPhone launch unleashed a wave of enthusiasm that Apple still surfs today: at the time of writing, Apple has just announced the largest quarterly earnings in the history of business.[1] And the use of threes was no coincidence. Jobs used the rule of three throughout his career, in every momentous statement he ever made, from the Mac launch in 1984 to his famous Stanford Commencement Address and his final launch of the iPad. Steve Jobs knew that three is the magic number.

Three is the magic number

The magic of the rule of three

Beanz Meanz Heinz. A Mars a day helps you work rest and play. Snap, Crackle and Pop. Education, education, education. No! No! No! Hip,

FIGURE 19.1 / **The power of three**

hip, hooray! Government of the people, by the people, for the people. This, that and the other. Location, location, location. See no evil, hear no evil, speak no evil. Head, thorax, abdomen. Animal, vegetable, mineral. Breakfast, lunch, supper. Past, present, future. Yeah, yeah, yeah. Yada, yada, yada. Bish, bash, bosh. Been there, seen it, done it. Health, wealth and happiness. *Liberté, égalité, fraternité.*

The rule of three is everywhere. It is extraordinary that one simple device has provided the basis for so many of the most memorable phrases, stories, songs, jokes and quotations in our language (Table 19.1). It is all over the place. Here, there and everywhere.

Four sounds over-the-top, hyperbolic, exaggerative and a bit bonkers. Two is too little, too measly. Three sounds decisive, complete and final. And, critically, it works. Academics have shown that that three-part claims are more persuasive than four-part claims.

Three-part claims are more persuasive

TABLE 19.1 Examples of the rule of three

Nursery Rhymes	Goldilocks and the Three Bears Three Blind Mice Three Little Pigs
Sport	On your marks... Get set... Go! Ready! Aim! Fire! Gold, silver, bronze
Music	Money, Money, Money Sex and Drugs and Rock 'n' Roll A,B,C, talking about 1,2,3
Films	*The Good, the Bad and the Ugly* *Planes, Trains and Automobiles* *Sex, Lies and Videotapes*
Film ads	Is it a bird, is it a plane, it's Superman! He's afraid, he's alone, he's 3 million light years from home. Lions, tigers and bears. Oh my!
Literature	Jam tomorrow, jam yesterday, but never jam today. Ghost of Christmas past, Christmas present and Christmas future. *The Lion, the Witch and the Wardrobe*
Comedy	Englishman, Irishman, Scotsman. Infamy! Infamy! They've all got it in for me! Sex and drugs and sausage roll!
Shakespeare	Romeo, Romeo, wherefore art thou Romeo? A horse! A horse! My kingdom for a horse! Some are born great, some achieve greatness, and some have greatness thrust upon them.
Religion	Father, Son and the Holy Ghost Faith, Hope and Charity Gold, Frankincense and Myrrh
Law	I promise to tell the truth, the whole truth and nothing but the truth. OJ Simpson could not, would not and did not commit this crime. Ready, aim, fire.
War	Never before has so much been owed by so many to so few. Now is not the end. It is not even the beginning of the end. But it is perhaps, the end of the beginning. Ein Volk! Ein Reich! Ein Führer!

Why the rule of three works

Why does the rule of three work? There are plenty of theories.

Some say it is because three is the earliest point at which a pattern can be detected. For instance, if I give you numbers 1 and 2, you could not say with confidence which number will come next. It could be 3 (if the pattern is rising by one), it could be 4 (if the pattern is doubling). It is only when the third point in the sequence is added that the pattern becomes clear. That is what gives the rule of three that conclusive feel, like the final nail in the argument.

Others say it is based on the ancient rhetorical idea of an enthymeme to prove a point. An enthymeme also involves three steps, for instance:

- Major premise – all men are mortal.
- Minor premise – Barack Obama is a man.
- Conclusion – therefore, Barack Obama is mortal.

I believe the rule of three works because of two factors, both of which are embedded deep in our brains. First, our bodily experience comes from being balanced (more on this in Chapter 20). This means we're used to comparing things between two extremes, such as left and right, forward and back, up and down. Given two extremes, the third point therefore represents the fulcrum, the midpoint between those two points. This makes it sound like the last word.

The second reason is familiarity. We are so used to hearing arguments made in threes throughout our lives that we develop a sense of expectation that arguments will conclude with a third.

We can speculate why it works but ultimately the most important thing is that it does. And it doesn't just work in language, threes are also found in art, music and design. This is why the grid on your camera viewer is broken up into a three by three grid. This is why plays are broken into three acts. This is why trilogies are so popular. Threes imply completeness, finality and perfection. Just. Like. That.

The rule of three in practice

So, how can you use the rule of three? Well, the chances are you already do: you just don't know it.

People naturally use the rule of three when they feel passionate. Check it out. Try to persuade someone to go to Malta – cheap beer, great beaches, short flight. Thank someone for their work: 'Good, good, good.' Commend someone on their performance: 'Efficient, reliable, committed.' Often, people add on a third even when none naturally arises, just to sound complete: on subsequent examination it is discovered that points two and three are actually identical, interchangeable and indistinguishable.

The trouble comes when people are speaking about things that they are not passionate about, but when they still need to be persuasive. In these cases, we can deliberately use the rule of three. We can contrive its occurrence and force it in all over the place: in conversations, emails, brochures and letters and particularly in speeches.

The rule of three and speeches

The rule of three is so common in speeches that it is hard even to think of any advice for speakers that does not come in threes: from the idea that a good speaker should 'stand up, speak up and shut up',[2] to the much-quoted but ill-founded advice that a good speaker should 'tell 'em what you're going to say, then tell 'em it, then tell 'em what you've just told 'em' (the presentation trainer Graham Davies says this is a bit like 'tell your audience you're going to patronise 'em, then patronise 'em, then tell 'em they've just been patronised').

The rule of three is also often used as a marker to signify the opening of a speech: from 'Friends, Romans, Countrymen' to 'My Lords, ladies and gentlemen', to the opening of Earl Spencer's eulogy to Diana, Princess of Wales at Westminster Abbey in 1997: 'I stand before you today, the representative of a family in grief, in a country in mourning, before a world in shock'. The rule of three also often signifies the end of a speech: 'So it's goodnight from him and it's goodnight from me. Goodnight'; 'Thank you, God Bless you and God Bless America'; 'Eat, drink and be merry'.

Many speeches are structured around threes: a beginning, a middle and an end (except if you're a philosopher, in which case it's usually a beginning, a muddle and an end). Ideas are often broken down into threes, to make them easy to swallow. For example: our past, our present and our future; better products, better service and better ideas; or the instinctive, the emotional and the logical.

The rule of three is also often used to create the soundbites in speeches. After Britain's 2010 general election, when the Labour and Conservative leaders were both wrangling with the Liberal Democrats to form a government, both sides were competing through rules of three. The Conservatives said they wanted to form a 'good, strong, stable government';[3] whilst Labour said they were looking to create a 'strong, stable and principled government'. The rule of three is great for soundbites. Just glance at the BBC News website now: I bet there are loads of threes in the quotes. As I write this, some of the biggest political stories of recent weeks have included David Cameron condemning the EU as 'too big, too bossy and too interfering', Alex Salmond condemning Westminster for 'bluff, bluster and bullying' and Boris Johnson condemning his party's 'splitters, quitters and kippers'.

There you go. Three examples. *Surely* you can't want more?

The rule of three and inspiration

Campaigns are often based around three messages. Bill Clinton's 1992 campaign was based upon: 'It's the economy, stupid', 'Change versus more of the same' and 'Don't forget health care'. Labour's message in the 2010 general election was 'Future, family and fairness', although mischievious Peter Mandelson joked it should be 'Futile, finished and fucked'. The three helps lodge the messages in the mind.

That's why many mission statements are also based upon a three. Starbucks serves 'one person, one cup, one neighbourhood', the BBC's mission is 'to inform, to educate and to entertain' whilst the US Marines' mission is 'Duty, honor and country'.[4] In fact, the US Marines even use threes organisationally. They use three-person teams; at one point, they experimented with fours and performance plummeted.

The rule of three works just as well one-to-one as it does with the big communication pieces. My daughters are crazy about Justin Fletcher, aka

Mr Tumble. I recently read an interview with him where he described meeting the CBeebies's commissioning editor, Ian Lockland, in the late 1990s. Lockland told him there were three secrets to children's television: clarity, contact and commitment.[5] What great leadership through a great rule of three: a rule of three so effective that it could still be remembered perfectly 16 years later. That's the Language of Leadership.

There's no getting away from the rule of three…

You can use the rule of three all over the place. If you're a teacher, break up your lessons into threes. If you're a salesperson, describe the benefits in threes. If you're an accountant, sum up the critical action points from the year's accounts in a three.

Threes are good for all of us, whether we're politicians like David Cameron, when he says:

> A modern compassionate Conservatism is right for our times, right for our party — and right for our country. If we go for it, if we seize it, if we fight for it with every ounce of passion, vigour and energy from now until the next election, nothing and no one can stop us.[6]

Or anti-politicians like Russell Brand:

> I'm not voting out of absolute indifference and weariness and exhaustion from the lies, treachery, deceit of the political class that has been going on for generations now, and has now reached fever pitch where we have a disenfranchised, disillusioned, despondent underclass that are not being represented by that political system.[7]

Three threes in one sentence. Powerful stuff. The one criticism might be that it's a little *too* forceful. It would be even more persuasive if it sounded more balanced, so let's move on to balance, the next element in the Language of Leadership.

chapter

20 Balance

'Style can be used to demonstrate balanced thought, rigorous thinking and show the completion of ideas.'

Demetrius

The perennial human quest for balance

One of the proudest moments in any parent's life comes when their children take their first steps. Months of effort, determination, banged heads, bruises and tantrums will have preceded this moment; but, at that point, the child gains one of the single most important traits required of mankind: balance.

Balance is essential to success in all parts of our lives. Balanced diets, balanced thoughts, balanced minds. Balance underpins science, maths and engineering. Balance is seen as something which is desirable in all the religions: Judaism, Islam, Buddhism and Christianity. We need balance to walk, run and swim. It's yin and yang, night and day, man and woman.

Balance is intrinsic to the human experience. Our whole bodies are designed around a need for balance. We have two eyes, two ears, two arms, two hands, two legs, two feet, and we have to get the balance between each of these right or we fall down – literally. Whilst I type this paragraph, my two hands work in balance. As you read this page, your two eyes scan the words and send information to your brain as if they were one eye. It's all about balance.

The embodiment theory in neuroscience states that our cognition is based on our bodily experience. If balanced bodies are good, so must balanced thoughts be good. That is why, in the Language of Leadership, the points we make must sound as if they are balanced. If an argument sounds balanced, we assume it is balanced.

If an argument sounds balanced, we assume it is balanced

Balanced arguments

The ancient Romans understood the importance of balance in arguments. Cicero advocated this structure for speeches:

1. Exposition – introduce the theme.
2. Narrative history – narrative factual history to date.
3. Division – the question faced today.
4. Evidence in support.
5. Refutation.
6. Summary.

This structure has an inbuilt balance. The way the argument develops sounds quasi-judicial, as if both sides of the argument are being weighed up before being concluded. That is why it is so effective and it is why so many leaders use this structure to sequence their argument. Let me illustrate by using this structure to tackle the often-controversial issue of nuclear power: making the case both for and against:

In favour of nuclear power:

1. Exposition – So… the next generation of energy supplies.
2. Narrative history – Since the dawn of time, man has actively sought out new forms of energy. As soon as new energy forms were

discovered, they were immediately put to use. Extracted, exploited. This is what happened with fire, coal and gas. It is what happened with tidal, solar and hydro energy. It is what people are proposing we do now with nuclear.

3. Division – But a question mark hangs over this.
4. Evidence – Compared to old fossil fuels, nuclear power is:
   (a) safer;
   (b) more secure;
   (c) more sustainable.
5. Refutation – Turning our back on nuclear will increase our dependence on old fossil fuels. Old fossil fuels are running out. They are also much higher in CO_2 emissions. Carrying on with business as usual is just not an option.
6. Summary – We should press on with new-build nuclear power stations without further delay.

Sounds convincing? But now let's flip it over, using the same structure.

Against nuclear power:

1. Exposition – We need an honest and balanced debate about nuclear power, not one dominated by the vested interests.
2. Narrative history – Throughout the last 70 years, successive governments have only ever talked about the positive benefits of nuclear energy. But do you remember Windscale? Chernobyl? Fukushima?
3. Division – Is it right that we press ahead?
4. Evidence – Nuclear power is:
   (a) dangerous;
   (b) damaging to the environment;
   (c) financially deadly – a ticking time bomb.
5. Refutation – Those with a financial interest in nuclear energy are putting out skewed reports and claiming they are independent. You can't trust them. To them, it's all about the money.
6. Summary – Let's get out of this toxic mess before we wind up facing a real disaster, not on another continent, but right here in Britain.

These are the bones of pretty good arguments. They need some flesh added but it would be easy to create a powerful 20-minute speech from these.

Let's try another subject. One issue that will certainly be debated over the coming years is Britain's membership of the European Union. So, in anticipation, how might the two camps put forward their arguments using Cicero's structure?

Against membership of the European Union:

1. Exposition – Thank God we've finally got this opportunity to discuss Britain's future.
2. Narrative history – Look, it's simple. The United Kingdom is stronger on its own.
   Always has been. Always will be. Look back through history – Henry VIII, Queen Victoria, Winston Churchill. We're a proud nation. We don't need the French. We don't need the Germans. The world looks to us for inspiration. We don't need to look to the world.
3. Division – This is a once-in-a-lifetime opportunity to decide once and for all: in or out.
4. Evidence – If we leave, we'll be once again free to set our own laws. Free to control our own borders. Free to say what we want on the global stage – a strong voice that is clearly and resolutely British.
5. Refutation – If we stay in, expect more of the same. More daft laws. More daft meetings. More daft proposals.
6. Summary – Don't hang about. Let's get out.

In favour of membership of the European Union:

1. Exposition – It's great we've got this opportunity to talk in a calm and considered way about Britain's relationship with Europe. The debate so far has involved too much heat, not enough light.
2. Narrative history – Let's just remember how the European Union came into being, shall we... Cast your mind back. The end of the Second World War. Europe lay in ruins; 40 million lives lost in 30 years. Great cities were reduced to rubble.
   But something good emerged from that rubble. The decision was made to tie together the economies of Europe. The rationale was clear: by tying together our economies, we would make war far less likely.

Since then, we've had 70 years of peace in Europe. We've had 70 years of rising prosperity.

3. Division – But now we are asked to put all this at risk.
4. Evidence – We know that being in Europe is good for our economy – 3 million jobs are linked to trade with Europe.

   We know that being in Europe is good for our environment – meaning we can work together to tackle climate change, pollution and waste.

   We know that being in Europe is good for our society too – working across borders to stop criminals and criminal activity.
5. Refutation – To turn our back on Europe now would be to try to turn the tide of history. It would be to turn back the clock to a time when Europe was divided and endangered. Who could want that?
6. Summary – Let's not give up on the EU. Let's make it better for you.

Most major modern political speeches follow the Cicero structure: consciously or not. It's a naturally logical sequence and one that is well received. Everyone recognises the 'on the one hand this, on the other hand that' emerging and it makes the argument easier to follow and more satisfying on conclusion

Modern political speeches follow the Cicero structure

Balanced sentences

Balanced sentences come in a variety of forms. The ancient Greek rhetoricians had names for all of these: the important thing is that, in appealing to the logical mind, the sentence has to sound balanced: it needs to be based upon that kind of see-saw feel. So, instead of just asserting, 'we must do x', we find an opposite, a point of contrast or a point of comparison to set it against. 'We're cutting taxes and raising growth.' 'We're reducing waste and increasing profitability.' 'We're cutting budgets and improving satisfaction.' These all sound balanced. They're not: they could actually represent diametrically opposed positions, but as long as they sound balanced, that is what matters (Table 20.1).

TABLE 20.1 Examples of balance

Balancing Formula	Examples
Not this… but that	Not flash but Gordon. Not surviving, but thriving.
This… not that	The state is your servant, not your master. There is such a thing as society, it's just not the same thing as the state. '*Mufrius, non magister*', which translates roughly as 'You're a gorilla, not a guru'.
This… or that	To be or not to be. You're either with us or you're against us. We must succeed or we will fail.
This statement is x number of words… That statement is x number of words	Science without religion is lame, religion without science is blind.
Not the opposite of x…, you're x	You're not with us, you're against us.
This… Followed by slight variation of this…	Tough on crime, tough on the causes of crime. Pro Europe, pro reform in Europe. If you want something said, ask a man; if you want something done, ask a woman. Ask not what your country can do for you, ask what you can do for your country. People are more impressed by the power of our example rather than by the example of our power.
Finish first part with one word, word then begins the second part	All you need is love, love is all you need.

Balance in practice

Balance often features in slogans, as shown in Table 20.2.

Balance is also important in politics. Third-way politics was actually all about balance – both rhetorically and politically. Triangulation involved finding a new middle point above two old orthodox positions.[1] This had instant appeal because most voters would consider themselves balanced.

In rhetorical terms, this led to many soundbites that combined the rule of three and balance, so 'it is not about over-regulation or deregulation, it's about the right regulation'. 'It is not about slavishly doing what is in the interests of the European Union or slavishly doing what is in the interests

TABLE 20.2   Balancing slogans

Product	Slogan
Mac Pro	Beauty outside. Beast inside.
Playstation 2	Live in your world. Play in ours.
Kodak	Share moments. Share life.
Walmart	Save money. Live Better.
Maltesers	Melt in your mouth, not in your hand.
Kit Kat	Have a break, have a Kit Kat.
KFC	Get a bucket of chicken, have a barrel of fun.
Maybelline	Maybe she's born with it, maybe it's Maybelline.
Harley-Davidson	American by birth. Rebel by choice.
Miller Beer	If you've got the time, we've got the beer.
Miss Clairol	Does she… Or doesn't she?
Sainsbury's	Good food costs less.

of the United States, it is about consistently doing what is in the interests of Britain'; or 'it is not about choosing between social justice and economic efficiency, it is about having a strong economy and a strong society'. So the third way was sensible politically and rhetorically: a double whammy.

Balance and speeches

Balanced statements often feature in speeches. Many great leaders open up their speeches with a whole series of balancing statements:

> 'We observe today not a victory of party, but a celebration of freedom – symbolising an end, as well as a beginning – signifying renewal, as well as change.'
>
> John F. Kennedy, Inaugural Speech, 1960

> 'Socialism stands for cooperation, not confrontation; for fellowship, not fear. It stands for equality, not because it wants people to be the same but because only through equality in our economic circumstances can our individuality develop properly.'
>
> Tony Blair, Maiden Speech, 1983

'It's the answer spoken by young and old, rich and poor, Democrat and Republican, black, white, Hispanic, Asian, Native American, gay, straight, disabled and not disabled.'

Barack Obama, Victory Speech, 2008

These kinds of openings always feel as if the leader is presenting themselves at the centre of the universe: omniscient and omnipotent; the central point in a world of extremes. It is the Language of Leadership.

Balance and inspiration

Balance is a common feature in many inspirational quotes and statements. In fact, the first-ever line in the first-ever book of aphorisms was a balancing statement, 'Life is short, art long.'[2] Still today, many of the pseudo-intellectual comments pasted on Facebook are balancing statements. It is that which gives the appearance of the sublime. It is only on closer examination, when your left brain gets to work analysing the meaning that you realise they're mostly a load of nonsense.

Alliteration and assonance

Alliteration can reinforce a sense of balance. British Budget statements are always based around alliterative pairs – from the 'pound in your pocket', a 'price worth paying', 'prudence for a purpose', through to the 'people's priorities', 'boom and bust', 'welfare to work' and so on. It is no surprise that balance should feature so prominently as surely the purpose of any budget is to balance the books. Gordon Brown loved alliterative pairs – 'listen and learn', 'challenge and change' and even his anthology of speeches was called 'The Change we Choose'. George Osborne has carried it forward: with the 'road to recovery', a 'Budget for Britain'

British Budget statements are always based around alliterative pairs and a choice between 'competence or chaos' at the 2015 election.[3] It's not just a British thing: much of the world now characterises the financial order as 'the new normal'.

Alliteration contains an inherent playfulness. It has been enjoyed by many of Britain's greatest writers, from Bunyan (*The Pilgrim's Progress*) to Shakespeare (*Love's Labour's Lost*) to The Beatles ('Magical Mystery Tour'). Alliteration is a great way to elevate balancing slogans to an even higher level – good to great, do or die, now or never, love it or loathe it, friend or foe, broke or bust, too little too late.

Not everyone warms to alliteration. Some avoid it completely, thinking it sounds too slick, too smart. Jimmy Carter's speechwriters said of him that he was the kind of guy who would say, 'That's the way the cookie falls apart.' Carter sounds a bit dull: he probably wouldn't even see anything sublime in a rhyme, which takes us on to the next essential element in the secret science of the Language of Leadership.

21 Rhyme or Reason

chapter

'Rosalind: But are you so much in love as your rhymes speak?
Orlando: Neither rhyme nor reason can express how much.'
William Shakespeare, *As You Like It*

The enduring powers of rhyme

In the early 1970s, Ronald Powell Bagguley, the head teacher of a small primary school in Derbyshire, wrote to the *Sunday Times* bemoaning the influence of television, calling for a return to good old-fashioned nursery rhymes. His letter was read by a musician in New York. The musician was so incensed he immediately fired off a response to the head teacher, via the newspaper. He said, instead of criticising, he should look at the positive ways rhymes could be used on television to promote learning: like *Sesame Street*, teaching children to read using jingles, just as the old nursery rhymes. The musician urged the head teacher to get with it. He signed off, cheekily quoting the Alka Seltzer ad: 'Try it, you'll like it'.

Nothing so extraordinary about that, but the musician in question was John Lennon. So one leader to another leader: disagreeing about the best medium for teaching children, but both of them agreed upon the importance of rhymes.

Rhymes make arguments more believable

Rhymes have long held a special role in education and persuasion. We've long been led to believe things are true if they rhyme. The phrase 'rhyme or reason' has been around since at least the 15th century, showing there have always been concerns that rhyme can appear to provide proof of reason. We now have research to prove this is true.

Studies show that people are more likely to believe something is true if it rhymes than if it does not rhyme. In one particular study, one half of a group of people was given rhyming sayings (such as 'caution and measure will win you treasure' or 'life is strife') whilst the other half was given statements that did not rhyme ('caution and measure will win you riches' or 'life is struggle').[1] The group with rhyming statements were more likely to believe their sayings than those who were not. Critically, they also denied that they were influenced by the rhyme. That makes rhyme all the more powerful: not only does it make claims more credible, people don't even realise they are being hoodwinked.

People are more likely to believe something is true if it rhymes

Rhymes tap deep into our minds

Nietzsche argued that rhymes had a vaguely magical quality, as if we are speaking with the Gods.[2] Rhymes probably remind us less of speaking with the gods than they do about speaking with our parents and our teachers. After all, when we're children, it is through rhyme that we learn the alphabet (abcdefg, hijklmnop...), about danger (Humpty Dumpty sat on the wall, Humpty Dumpty had a great fall) and even about how to get dressed in the morning (One, two, buckle my shoe).

These patterns and rhythms imprint on our minds at the very earliest age. There was some research that showed we pick up on such rhythmic patterns literally when we are in the womb. Babies who were played 'The Cat in the Hat' in the womb would, after they were born, actively seek out poems which followed that same rhythm.[3]

Rhymes just sound believable. The words sound as if they naturally fit together, so we assume that they do naturally fit together.

Practical use of rhymes

So what do you do with this insight? Now I'm not proposing you go around speaking in rhyme: whilst that would almost certainly win you attention, it wouldn't *necessarily* be the kind of attention a leader wants. What I propose instead is that you might perhaps try to use rhyme when you can't afford for your message to miss. Like threes, rhymes are great for creating seriously striking soundbites and slogans.

Use rhyme when you can't afford for your message to miss

As is shown in Table 21.1, many of the greatest advertising slogans in history have rhymed.

Many delivery vehicles have rhymes emblazoned upon the side, from 'You shop, we drop' to 'From our store to your door' and 'Short on time? Shop online'. Nice rhymes.

TABLE 21.1   **Rhyming slogans**

Product	Slogan
Timex	Takes a licking, keeps on ticking.
Ford	Everything we do, is driven by you.
Gillette	Gillette, the best a man can get.
Mars	A Mars a day helps you work rest and play.
Budweiser	For all you do. This Bud's for you.
Kwik Fit	You can't get better than a Kwik Fit fitter.
Haig Whisky	Don't be vague, ask for Haig.

Business people can use rhymes to sum up their philosophies. Richard Branson has 'screw it, let's do it'. Jack Welch had a 'rank and yank' strategy for getting rid of the bottom 10% of his company.

We can pitch questions in rhymes. Are we working 'smarter or harder?' What do you think – hot or not? Do you prefer a 'tree book or an ebook?' Will you send 'email or snail mail?'

Rhymes can also prove good for creating memorable models. Tuckman's description of the stages of teams as 'forming, storming, norming, performing' is an example of a model where the rhyme surpasses the reason. In my experience, this model is better remembered than it is understood – everyone I've ever asked has a very flaky conception of what norming and storming actually mean, but they go with it because the rhyme makes it sound so damn simple. It's more about the rhyme than the reason.

Rhymes can also work well in speeches. Sometimes they slip in very discreetly, almost beneath the radar. In 2014, David Cameron closed his party conference speech with three discreet rhymes in direct succession:

> 'History is written by us, in the decisions we make today and that starts next May.
>
> So Britain: what's it going to be?
>
> I say: let's not go back to square <u>one</u>. Let's finish what we have <u>begun</u>.
>
> Let's build a Britain we are proud to call home......for you, for your family, for everyone'.

These rhymes were almost imperceptible: at least, there was no comment on them in the following days' press. But they were present nonetheless, and would have discreetly made his message just that bit more palatable.

Sometimes the rhyme can be move overt. Muhammad Ali once made a speech at Harvard University. It was characteristically inspiring. At one point, he paused to take a breath. A student shouted out, 'Go on

Muhammad, give us one of your poems.' Ali paused. He leaned into the microphone. 'Me? We.'

Beautiful. The Language of Leadership. Use it, don't abuse it. If you can't use it, lose it. It's up to you to do what you do. And what you do depends on your perspective…

chapter 22

Power of Perspective

In 1773, James Boswell took Samuel Johnson to Edinburgh, to show off his home city. They wandered down one of those narrow old Georgian alleys, just a couple of metres wide when they looked up and saw two women leaning out of their windows shouting angrily at one another, waving their brooms across the alley. Dr Johnson pointed at the women: 'Those two women will never agree', said the great man, 'because they are arguing from different premises.'

The place we start an argument from has a crucial bearing on where we finish. I was a massive fan of the TV series *Yes Minister* in the 1980s. I used to love watching Sir Humphrey Appleby twist Jim Hacker around his little finger. For light relief, look on YouTube for the scene where Sir Humphrey demonstrates to Bernard how polling companies construct lines of questioning to elicit particular responses by starting from different positions (https://www.youtube.com/watch?v=G0ZZJXw4MTA). The sketch is funny but the point is serious.

Most people in life do not have a fixed view on most issues. Rather, they have floating positions based on shifting perspectives. Changing people's perspectives is the key to changing their positions.

Changing people's perspectives is the key to changing their positions

Great leaders deliberately control perspective. They often start from a point of universal agreement: a point with which people will find it very hard to disagree. Having started from a base of agreement, they then slowly move forward from there. The more strongly the opening point is believed, the more effective the appeal.

Against a cap on banker bonuses:

- Do you believe the government should have the power to tell you what to do with your money?
- Do you believe the government should have the power to tell anyone what to do with their money?
- Do you believe the government should be able to dictate how much money people are paid?
- Do you believe the government should cap bonuses in certain arbitrarily selected sectors?
- Do you believe bankers' bonuses should be capped?

In favour of a cap on banker bonuses:

- Do you believe failure should be rewarded?
- Do you believe the banks should be subsidised with hundreds of billions of pounds of public money whilst nurses and doctors are getting pay cuts?
- Do you believe it is right that the banks are using these subsidies to still pay out multi-million-pound bonuses to the same people who caused the crash?
- Do you believe government should veer away from standing up to powerful vested interests?
- Do you believe bankers' bonuses should be capped?

The insight is that people do not like looking inconsistent, unprincipled or selfish: that is how you can get people to continue agreeing, even if you move the argument on to places they previously would have found objectionable. If the answer to the first and second question is 'yes' then surely the answer to the third question is also likely to be 'yes'. Every slick salesperson knows the power of getting people nodding. Once people start nodding, they find it difficult to stop. It's what is known as a heuristic, a rule of thumb, but it is a flawed way of thinking.

Once people start nodding, they find it difficult to stop

Research showed that, when people were asked to place a large sign in their gardens that said 'Drive Safely', most refused. If, however, they were first asked about their community-mindedness, then they agreed. Just think how the same approach could be put to work for you: if you start your argument from deeply felt, universally agreed values statements. It's all about creating patterns.

Getting the mood right

Perspective is not just about the argument. Sometimes, it's just about getting the mood right. In Tony Blair's book *The Journey*, he describes how he handled the Northern Ireland peace talks. These negotiations must rank amongst the most difficult of recent history. But Blair's approach was simple: he made it his mission every morning to get people nodding. He knew that if he got people nodding just once, he would break that stubborn rick in the back of their necks. So he'd make some vague statement – 'There are tough issues to deal with today' or 'Isn't the weather awful' or 'Wasn't yesterday tricky?' – it didn't matter; as soon as he'd got the first nod, the path was clear to move on to more substantive issues.

Getting right the when, where and what

There are a range of other factors that also affect perspective.

I once worked with a major automotive company that wanted to run its Language of Leadership workshop in a park. Their company has a simple theory: fresh thinking requires fresh perspectives. It was a great day: the open vistas led to some real open thinking; the smell of fresh grass led to more positivity; the contact with the outside world created greater openness. Perspective was changed. It was great. A definite success.

If you want to speak to someone about the future, why not talk about it when you're experiencing some forward motion. Research has shown that people are more likely to think about the future when they are experiencing even the slightest movement; on a train or even just standing in a post office queue. If you are discussing someone's career or personal development, discuss it when you're on the move. They will be literally and metaphorically forward-focused.

Be aware of how mood affects people's view. What hormones are flowing in their brain: cortisol, oxytocin, dopamine or serotonin? If you catch someone just after they've finished a vigorous game of sport then you will find them feeling strong, powerful, confident and calm. Imagine what you could get them to do in this state of mind? Conversely, taking someone out for a slap-up lunch – wining and dining them – is likely to put them in the wrong state for taking on new responsibilities: they'll be thinking about when they can grab 40 winks.

Timing also fundamentally affects perspective. People are more likely to think about their future at the end of the week than they are at the beginning. This is why almost all email mailshots take place on Fridays. It makes you wonder, though, why most team meetings are held on Mondays – as 50% of employees get into work late on Mondays and then spend an average of 12 minutes complaining. They're 100% sure to respond negatively to new suggestions, aren't they? Oh, and 97% of stats are made up on the spot. And 74% of these are exaggerated... Speaking of stats...[1]

23

Think of a Number

'There are three types of lies – lies, damned lies and statistics.'
Benjamin Disraeli

People don't understand numbers

Peter Mandelson once said that most people don't understand statistics or, if they do, they think that they are bullshit. He had a point. Half of British adults do not have the mathematical skills expected of an 11 year old.[1] Numbers just don't work for a lot of people. I've worked with high-profile people who regularly confused millions and billions, even in press conferences: most of the time, the journalists didn't notice either. Research shows that the brain is only capable of processing seven bits of data at a time.[2] Nevertheless, so many modern leaders think you're not leading effectively if you don't have a never-ending blitzkrieg of stats up your sleeve.

Half of British adults do not have the mathematical skill expected of an 11 year old

How leaders use stats effectively

Use numbers only to create powerful impressions and images

The Language of Leadership does not unleash numbers for the sake of it. We use numbers only to create powerful impressions and images: that is how they gain power.[3] Impressions and images are the things that stick.

Here are some of the ways we can do that.

Building a rhythm

You can build a rhythm. 'Investment is up. Growth is up. Employment is up. House prices are up. Trade is up.' Keep this going long enough, using the rhetorical device of repetition, and before you know it the crowd gets so intoxicated with all the dopamine that they start spontaneously applauding: if they do, just surf the waves and keep the ups coming. We do not need to be specific, it's all about making impressions.

Finding persuasive points of comparison

You can adjust perspective. Statistics and numbers mean nothing on their own – it is only in relation to other numbers that they acquire meaning. You want to put your number up against something that makes it appear either incredibly large or incredibly small.

So, in the Language of Leadership, we carefully pick points of comparison that enhance our case: in the same way as discount retailers do with their 70%-off stickers.

Table 23.1 shows how different points of contrast create vastly different perceptions of scale, dramatically altering our perspective.

Let's take a specific issue: the TV licence fee in Britain. Is it good value or not? In Table 23.2 we look at both sides of this argument, distorting perspective on each side to strengthen our case.

Throwing in a story as well will make your stat even more sticky. A story and stat combined can create two powerful images. So, if you were making

TABLE 23.1   Distorting statistics

Question	Neutral Stat	Distorted to seem High	Distorted to seem Low
Is executive pay too high?	The average FTSE CEO pay is £4.4 million.	This is 120 times the average salary of their workers.[1]	This is just 0.5% on average of their company profits.[2]
Is crime out of control?	There were 489,045 burglaries in the UK in 2012.	Every year there's a burglary in every street in Britain.[3]	The number of burglaries has fallen 45% since 2002.[4]
Is motorcycling too dangerous?	317 motorcyclists die in accidents in the UK every year.	Every day, somewhere in Britain, a motorcyclist dies.	Every year 300 times as many people die from lung cancer and respiratory diseases than on motor bikes.

[1] http://www.cipd.co.uk/pm/peoplemanagement/b/weblog/archive/2013/09/23/median-pay-for-ftse-100-chief-execs-at-163-4-4-million.aspx (accessed 27 January 2015).
[2] http://www.haygroup.com/downloads/uk/Exec_pay_in_persective_press_release.pdf (accessed 27 January 2015).
[3] https://www.gov.uk/government/publications/household-interim-projections-2011-to-2021-in-england (accessed 27 January 2015).
[4] *Facts are Sacred*, Guardian guidebook.

TABLE 23.2   Licence fee – value for money or not?

The Licence Fee is Good Value	The Licence Fee is not Good Value
The licence fee costs just 40p a day, the price of a tin of beans.	Licence payers stump up £3.6 billion for the BBC every year, enough for 250 new schools.
The licence fee is one-third of the price of a Sky subscription.	Netflix is less than half the price of the licence fee.
Funding for the BBC is 25% lower in real terms over this charter period, so we only have £3 for every £4 we had in the past.	The BBC wasted £100 million on a digital library project that had to be junked – more than the entire value of Channel 5.

the case that the BBC licence fee was tremendously small, you might talk about an elderly relative, on their own in a small flat, listening to Radio 4 every day: for that person it is a lifeline. If you were making the case that the licence fee was tremendously large, you might talk about some of the payoffs that were put in the back pockets of retiring directors.

Graphics

Graphics can also help to create an image that will stick. One speechwriter I know who used to prepare presentations for a senior businessman told me that every single graph he prepared always had to follow the same 45-degree trajectory, at his boss's instruction. It didn't matter whether it was measuring growth, investment or jobs, just as long as it went up by a 45-degree angle. This was all about adjusting the axis to show a positive image: the brain naturally assumes that left to right and down to up is good.

Modern graphic design software presents enormous opportunities. Personally, I am a huge fan of Prezi (www.prezi.com). With Prezi, you can show a graphic of 100 people and then shade out parts of that group to illustrate percentages. You can then zoom in to one of them to tell a video story.

Less is more

Less is almost certainly more when it comes to statistics. A simple startling statistic can have much greater impact than a dozen stats in rapid succession. Every single person in this room owes £28,000; 24,000 children die every day from malnutrition; 1.2 billion people live on less than a dollar a day. These stats can explode in an audience like grenades.

Short contrasting stats can also prove powerful points. Apple has more cash than the US Reserve. The US spends more on its military than the next 19 countries on the list put together. The US spends more on its military than it does on its schools.

Attention will also be grabbed by stats that confound people's expectations: most murders are committed by someone known to the victim; there is a 65% chance that the love of your life will cheat on you.

But that's enough. I've already written far more stats than you can possibly remember. Damn. I should have followed my own advice and kept it simple. But we're almost at the end… There's just one more chapter left to cover in the Language of Leadership. Just one more point to make. I can't blinking remember what it was though…

chapter **24**

Brevity

'Sorry I'm writing you a long letter but I didn't have time to write you a short one.'

Mark Twain

Oh yeah. That's it. Keep it brief.

Epilogue

T.S. Eliot said that the end of our exploring is to arrive where we started and know the place for the first time.[1] So let's return to the two images that started this book: on the one hand, the disillusionment apparent in the Red Lion in today's leaders; on the other hand, the sheer joy and elation shared by 250,000 Londoners in Hyde Park in summer 2012.

What kind of leader do you want to be? Do you want to be the kind of leader who hangs over people like a dark cloud, bringing fear and shame, creating division and disenchantment? Or do you want to be the kind of leader who is like a bright light, offering clarity of vision, making people feel alive, inspired and invigorated?

If you have been given the title of leader, people expect you to lead. Look into their eyes and you will see them saying: 'Please be on my side. Please value me. Please make me feel good. Don't be like the rest. Don't let me down. Don't lie and cheat.' Give people what they need and they will give you what you need: their support. If you can't meet people's needs then you're probably not a leader, you're just someone with a job title.

You have a responsibility to care for the people who look to you. Most people don't care about their leaders because their leaders don't really care about them. They don't offer them security, they don't offer them love, they don't offer them purpose. This leaves a void. People are self-medicating to fill that void. Millions of people are on Prozac. We are all addicted to our phones. In the last year, we reached a tipping point: we now spend more time on our phones in the day than we do not on our phones. The average person picks up and starts tapping on their phone 110 times every day:[2] they are chasing the dopamine, oxytocin and serotonin of a Facebook like or a Twitter follow. People are desperately trying to fill the void in their lives.

Don't let them down. Give them pride. Give them purpose. Give them direction. This book contains a mass of ways in which you can meet people's needs: instinctively, emotionally and logically. You might not want to use all of these techniques: that is fine. Take a look around, take what you want, leave the rest behind. But don't underestimate their power. I've worked with leaders who have been suddenly thrust into positions of power – going from relatively hidden back-room jobs into positions of responsibility where literally millions of people are looking to them – and I've seen the difference these techniques can make: telling stories, empathising, changing perspectives. Once leaders discover the Language of Leadership, there is no going back. As soon as they see the effect the techniques have, they then use them over and over again.

If you give people what they need, then they will give you the support you need. And with that support behind you, who knows what you will go on to achieve in the world.

Acknowledgements

On 24 October 2008, I ran a Creative Speechwriting workshop in London. I remember the day well. It was an exciting time: just after the birth of my first daughter and just before the US elected its first black president. On that day, I met Anna Jones, then head of internal communications at the Big Lottery Fund. It was Anna who first saw the possibility for offering speechwriting training within a leadership development programme. I am so grateful to her, together with Perry 'Punk HR' Timms and Peter 'Social CEO' Wanless, for giving me the spur to create what has since become one of the most sought-after communication workshops in the world.

The Language of Leadership workshop has taken me around the world. I have had so much fun – I love my work so much – and along the way I have met some incredibly inspiring people and it has been a privilege to help them tell their stories. I am so grateful to everyone who's attended one of the workshops, along with Paul Bennett and Mark Swain at Henley Business School, Sue Douthwaite at Cass Business School and Sarah Burton at the University of Cambridge for the huge backing which they have given to the Language of Leadership.

As far as the book is concerned, thanks to the team at Palgrave Macmillan, particularly Tamsine O'Riordan, Stephen Partridge and Josie Taylor. Thanks to Paul Rainey for the illustrations, Nicolai Lorenzen for the photograph and Tom Clark from *The Guardian* for his sage and friendly advice throughout the writing.

I couldn't have begun to write the book were it not for my family: my mum, who instilled in me a love of language from the earliest age and who went through three drafts of this book with the most phenomenal eye for detail; my dad, who checked the final proofs of the book from Japan; my brother, for being the best brother I've ever had; my daughters, who gave me the space to write when I could have been taking them to Legoland; and, in particular, my lovely wife, Lucy, whom I still adore after 11 years of marriage. Lucy is the leader in my life.

Readers – if you enjoy this book at all, it will be in no small part because of all the guff that Lucy struck out.

As usual with books like this, whilst I've made every effort to reference and seek permissions, if you spot an error or omission please let me know and I'll put it right. And if you are interested in sharing thoughts about the Language of Leadership, please do get in touch. Tweet me, email me. I'd love to hear from you.

Simon Lancaster

9 February 2015

Westminster, London

Email: simon@bespokespeeches.com

Twitter: @bespokespeeches

Original illustrations by Paul Rainey: pbrainey.com

Author photograph by Nicolai Lorenzen: www.nicolailorenzen.com

Notes

Introduction

1. Prozac is an SSRI: a Selective Serotonin Reuptake Inhibitor, an antidepressant that works by altering the levels of serotonin in the brain. Prozac was the first branded SSRI when it was first launched in 1988. By 2005, it was the most prescribed drug in the US. Today, there are several SSRIs prescribed in the UK including Faverin, Cipramil, Seroxat and Lustral. See http://www. nhs.uk/conditions/SSRIs-(selective-serotonin-reuptake-inhibitors)/Pages/ Introduction.aspx. Accessed 5/2/2015.

1   Winning Minds – The Secret Science of the Language of Leadership

1. The World Economic Forum surveys the 1500 or so members of its Global Agenda Council in advance of its annual meeting in Davos, Switzerland, to identify the critical issues facing the world. The 2015 survey put a 'lack of leadership' as the top three issue facing the world, after deepening income inequality and persistent jobless growth; 86% of respondents agreed that there is a leadership crisis in the world today. Trust is a critical issue. On a scale of 0 to 10, 0 being no confidence at all and 10 being complete confidence, leaders of non-profit and charitable organizations were the only sector to score more than 5. Every other sector scored less than 5. The lowest scoring sector, scoring even less than business, political and media leaders, was religious leaders. See http://reports.weforum.org/outlook-global-agenda-2015/top-10-trends- of-2015/3-lack-of-leadership/. Accessed 5/2/2015.
2. There are numerous surveys of trust at a national and global level. The most important one in the UK is the Ipsos MORI Veracity Index which has rated trust in a number of critical professions going back to 1983. The question is whether you trust (insert profession) to generally tell the truth or not. In 2014, just 16% of people trusted politicians to tell the truth whilst 32% of

people trusted business leaders to tell the truth. See https://www.ipsos-mori. com/researchpublications/researcharchive/15/Trust-in-Professions.aspx. Accessed 5/2/2015.

Edelman PR carry out a global survey of the state of trust around the world. The 2015 Edelman Trust Barometer showed a global decline in trust over the last year and the number of countries with trusted institutions has fallen to an all-time low among the informed public. See http://www.edelman.com/ insights/intellectual-property/2015-edelman-trust-barometer/trust-around-world. Accessed 5/2/2015.

3. Gallup's State of the Global Workplace Report. This describes engaged employees as people who work with passion and feel a profound connection to their company. They drive innovation and move the organization forward. Not-engaged employees are essentially 'checked out'. They're sleepwalking through the day, putting in time but not passion to their work. Actively disengaged employees aren't just unhappy at work; they're busy acting out their unhappiness. Every day, these workers undermine what their engaged co-workers accomplish. See http://www.gallup.com/businessjournal/166667/ five-ways-improve-employee-engagement.aspx. Accessed 5/2/2015.

4. OFCOM, the UK communications industry regulator, publishes an annual report on media use and attitudes. For several years now, this has shown an extraordinary growth in the amount of media use across a range of devices. See http://stakeholders.ofcom.org.uk/market-data-research/other/research-publications/adults/adults-media-lit-14/. Accessed 5/2/2015.

5. The figure for how much more powerful the emotional brain is than the logical brain varies from somewhere between five times more powerful (Jonas Ridderstrale and Kjelle Nordstrom) and twenty times as powerful (Lance Rennka). Suffice to say, it is much more powerful, given its ability to produce these powerful chemicals.

6. Charles Darwin in *The Expression of the Emotions in Man and Animals* (1872) said that there were six principal human emotions: anger, fear, sadness, disgust, surprise and enjoyment. In 2004, Simon Baron-Cohen produced an interactive emotions library on CD-ROM, which detailed 412 separate emotions. Simon Baron-Cohen (2004), *Mind Reading: The Interactive Guide to Emotions*, London: Jessica Kingsley Publishers.

7. Malcolm Gladwell (2006), *Blink: The Power of Thinking Without Thinking*, London: Penguin.

8. This research found that one-tenth of a second was enough for people to form an impression of someone's face. Giving someone a greater amount of exposure to someone's face did not significantly change the reaction. See Janine Wills and Alexander Todorov (2005), First Impressions: Making Up Your Mind After a 100-Ms Exposure to a Face, *Pyschological Science*, Princeton University,

NJ, available at http://psych.princeton.edu/psychology/research/todorov/pdf/Willis%26Todorov-PsychScience.pdf. Accessed 5/2/2015.

9. The faces of 40 female and 40 male students were rated for trustworthiness. Eye colour had a significant effect. The brown-eyed faces were perceived as more trustworthy than the blue-eyed faces. This was found to be down to the face shapes correlated with brown eyes rather than the colour of the eyes per se. See Karel Kleisner, Lenka Priplatova, Peter Frost and Jaroslav Flegr (2013), *Trustworthy-Looking Face Meets Brown Eyes*, Public Library of Science, available at http://journals.plos.org/plosone/article?id=10.1371/journal.pone.0053285. Accessed 5/2/2015.

10. Ilfat Maoz (2012), The Face of the Enemy: The Effect of Press-reported Visual Information Regarding the Facial Features of Opponent Politicians on Support for Peace, *Political Communication*, 01/2014, 31 (1), pp. 149–67. Available at http://www.researchgate.net/publication/239798108_The_Face_of_the_Enemy_The_Effect_of_Press-Reported_Visual_Information_Regarding_the_Facial_Features_of_Opponent_Politicians_on_Support_for_Peace. Accessed 5/2/2015.

11. Ben Jones and Lisa DeBruine, based in the Institute of Neuroscience and Pyschology at the University of Glasgow, have established the Face Research Lab. They have carried out all sorts of experiments about face preferences. You can take part in little online experiments yourself at: www.faceresearch.org.

12. This research was based upon the facial appearance of candidates in gubernatorial elections, the most important elections in the US after the presidential election. Charles C. Ballew II and Alexander Todorov (2007), Predicting Political Elections from Rapid and Unreflective Face Judgements, *PNAS*, 2007, Vol. 104, No. 46.

13. Simon Lancaster (2010), *Speechwriting, The Expert Guide*, London: Robert Hale.

14. James Geary, *Metaphorically Speaking*, available at ted.com. Accessed 5/2/2015. There are, however, even disagreements amongst experts in metaphor about what exactly constitutes a metaphor, because metaphors can creep into our language and become words. For instance, when we are talking about the 'brow' of a hill or the 'foothills of the Himalayas', would these constitute metaphors? Some would say not: they are just words. However, to me, they do suggest an image of personification – that the hill is a person – so they should be considered metaphors. What about words like propaganda? The root origin of the word propaganda is based on a metaphorical idea: that of ideas as seeds – propaganda propagates and spreads those ideas so they grow. Whatever, the important thing is that metaphors occur far more frequently than most people would imagine.

15. The Anti-Defamation League carries out regular surveys on occurrences in the Middle East. This survey was based on 1200 interviews carried out in October 2011. Available at: http://archive.adl.org/israel/adl-2011-middle-east-11.9.11.pdf. Accessed 5/2/2015.

16. Dr William Casebeer and Dr Paul Zac, *Empathy, Neurochemistry and the Dramatic Arc*, Futureofstorytelling.org. Watch the video at: https://www.youtube.com/watch?v=DHeqQAKHh3M. Accessed 5/2/2015.

17. Ian Sample, 'Brain scan sheds light on secrets of speech', *The Guardian*, 3 February 2004. Available at: http://www.theguardian.com/uk/2004/feb/03/science.highereducation. Accessed 5/2/2014.

18. Suzanne B. Shut and Kurt A. Carlson (2013), When Three Charms but Four Alarms: Identifying the Optimal Number of Claims in Persuasion Settings, *Social Science Research Network*, available at: http://www.anderson.ucla.edu/faculty/suzanne.shu/Shu%20Carlson%20Three%20in%20Persuasion.pdf. Accessed 5/2/2015.

19. Recently there has been a wealth of research showing the primacy of the instinctive mind. Nobel Prize-winner Daniel Kahneman's work has been at the forefront of this research. I highly recommend his book (2011) *Thinking Fast and Slow*, St Ives: Allen Lane. Jonathan Haidt's excellent book – (2012) *The Righteous Mind: Why Good People are Divided by Politics and Religion*, St Ives: Allen Lane – also contains fascinating, often hilarious, examples of how the instinctive brain can deceive. The APET model shows how the instinctive brain goes first: the sequence is:
    (i)   A – an activating agent, i.e. a stimulus of some description;
    (ii) P – pattern, i.e. the instinctive mind works out whether this is good or bad;
    (iii) E – emotion, i.e. the essential emotional responses are triggered and hormones will be released, if appropriate;
    (iv) T – thought, i.e. the cognitive process that results in active thought about what would be an appropriate response.

1   Winning the Instinctive Mind

1. Evian Gordon (2000), *Integrative Neuroscience: Bringing Together Biological, Psychological and Clinical Models of the Human Brain*, Ohio: CRC Press.

2. David Eagleman (2011), *Incognito – The Secret Lives of the Brain*, Chatham: Canongate, p. 5.

3. http://allaboutstevejobs.com/sayings/stevejobsanecdotes_all.php. Accessed 3/2/2015.

4. Richard Restak (2009), *The Naked Brain*, New York: Three Rivers Press, p. 216.
5. Sandra Blakeslee, Cells that Read Minds. Available at http://www.nytimes.com/2006/01/10/science/10mirr.html?pagewanted=all&_r=0. Accessed 3/2/2015.
6. Eric Hoffer (2006), *The Passionate State of Mind: And Other Aphorisms*, Titusville, NJ: Hopewell Publications.
7. David Brooks (2011), *The Social Animal*, Suffolk: Short Books.
8. There is a lot of fabulous further reading about the power of images in the instinctive mind. Two books which I would instantly recommend are George Lakoff (2004), *Don't Think of an Elephant: Know Your Values and Frame the Debate: The Essential Guide for Progressives*, Vermont: Chelsea Green; and Eamonn Holmes (2004), *Drop the Pink Elephant: 15 Ways to Say What You Mean... and Mean What You Say*, Oxford: Capstone.
9. 'President Obama, Elizabeth Warren have different message on the middle class' by Steven Mufson, Karen Tumulty and Anne Gearan. Available at http://www.washingtonpost.com/business/economy/president-obama-elizabeth-warren-share-different-message-on-the-middle-class/2015/01/07/8c0eb516-9681-11e4-8005-1924ede3e54a_story.html. Accessed 3/2/2015.

2   Metaphors that Move Minds

1. George Lakoff (1981), *Metaphors We Live By*, Chicago: University of Chicago Press.
2. *The Guardian*'s 'Great Speeches of the 20th Century' (2008) contained an excerpt from the Wind of Change speech along with some commentary from former Foreign Secretary, Douglas Hurd. Available at http://www.theguardian.com/world/series/great-speeches-harold-macmillan. Accessed 3/2/2015.
3. Michael W. Morris, Oliver J. Sheldon, Daniel R. Ames and Maia J. Young (2005), Metaphors and the market: Consequences and preconditions of agent and object metaphors in stock market commentary, Columbia Business School. Available at http://www1.gsb.columbia.edu/mygsb/faculty/research/pubfiles/2205/2005%2Epdf. Accessed 3/2/2015.
4. Charlie Cooper, Mind your language: 'Battling' cancer metaphors can make terminally ill patients worse, *The Independent*, 3 November 2014. Available at http://www.independent.co.uk/life-style/health-and-families/health-news/mind-your-language-battling-cancer-metaphors-can-make-terminally-ill-patients-worse-9836322.html. Accessed 3/2/2015.
5. This report was prepared confidentially for the Department of Health by McKinsey. It was leaked to *The Times* in 2009, creating quite some controversy.

The new Coalition government decided to publish the full report in 2010. You can view it here: http://www.nhshistory.net/mckinsey%20report.pdf. Accessed 4/2/2015.

6. Jonathan Charteris-Black (2001), A comparative, corpus-based study of figuration and metaphor in English and Malay phraseology. PhD thesis. University of Birmingham.

7. Adam Smith (1985), *Lectures on Rhetoric and Belles Lettres*, ed J.C. Bryce, vol. IV of the Glasgow edition of the works and correspondence of Adam Smith, Indianapolis: Liberty Fund.

8. Iain MacRury (2009), *Advertising*, London: Routledge.

9. Martin Lindstrom (2009), *Buyology: How Everything We Believe About Why We Buy Is Wrong*, London: Random House.

10. Available at http://www.robots.newcastle.edu.au/~chalup/chalup_publications/p045.pdf. Accessed 4/2/2015.

11. http://library.perdana.org.my/Speech_ab/TR1965.pdf. Accessed 20/4/2015.

3   The Look of Leadership

1. Available at http://www.bakadesuyo.com/2011/11/do-we-pick-leaders-based-on-their-voice/. Accessed 4/2/2015.

2. Sigmund Freud (1997), *Dora: An Analysis of a Case of Hysteria*, New York: Touchstone Books.

3. Roald Dahl (1980), *The Twits*, London: Jonathan Cape.

4. Jonathan Charteris-Black (2007), *The Communication of Leadership: The Design of Leadership Style*, Bolton: Routledge.

4   Inner Purpose

1. Alvin Ung (2012), *Barefoot Leader: The Art and Heart of Going That Extra Mile,* Malaysia: August Publishing.

2. Companies Act 2006.

3. Dan Pink (2010), *Drive: The Surprising Truth About What Motivates Us*, Chatham: Canongate.

4. Jim Collins and Jerry Porras (1994), *Built to Last: Successful Habits of Visionary Companies*, London: HarperBusiness.

5   Empathy and the Power of Nice

1. David Brooks, *The Social Animal*, p. 134.

2. Simon Baron-Cohen.

3. James W. Pennebaker (2011), *The Secret Life of Pronouns: What Our Words Say About Us*, Pennsylvania: Bloomsbury Press.

4. Shelley Taylor (2002), *The Tending Instinct*, New York: Henry Holt and Company.
5. Available at http://www.dailymail.co.uk/news/article-2251762/NRA-cond emned-astonishing-response-Sandy-Hook-massacre-calling-schools-arm-themselves.html. Accessed 12/2/2015.

6   Smiles and Humour

1. S. Hazeldine (2014), *Neuro-Sell: How Neuroscience Can Power Your Sales Success*, Croydon: Kogan Page, p. 24.
2. M. Sonnby–Borgström (2002), Automatic Mimicry Reactions as Related to Differences in Emotional Empathy, *Scandinavian Journal of Psychology*, Vol. 43, pp. 433–43.
3. A study of 14,500 HR directors. http://www.amazon.co.uk/Comedy-Writing-Secrets-2nd-Edition/dp/1582973571. Accessed 27/1/2015.
4. Available at http://books.google.co.uk/books?id=jmv2boghHzoC&pg=PT10 &lpg=PT10&dq=rhymes+in+persuasion&source=bl&ots=dWWndOC6A4&sig= HyNcGe9xOo6UGPiArOS9VCw7Ojc&hl=en&sa=X&ei=jObWUfvsGJOShgen1l C4Cw&ved=0CCwQ6AewADgU. Accessed 4/2/2015.
5. S. Freud (2014 [1905]), *Jokes and Their Relationship to the Unconscious*, London: White Press.
6. Daniel Goleman (2013), Primal Leadership: Unleashing the Power of Emotional Intelligence, *Harvard Business Review*, p. 11.
7. Research by Robert Provine, Professor of Psychology and Neuroscience at the University of Maryland.
8. That's according to analysis of 40,000 jokes by Professor Richard Wiseman.
9. John Lewis boss insults in two languages, by Jim Armitage, *The Independent*, 4 October 2014. Available at http://www.independent.co.uk/news/business/news/john-lewis-boss-insults-in-two-languages-9774248.html. Accessed 4/2/2015.

7   Breathing

1. James W. Pennebaker (1990), *Opening Up: The Healing Power of Expressing Emotions*, New York: Guilford Press, p. 178.

8   Style

1. Jon Oberlander and Alastair J. Gill (2005), Language with character: a stratified corpus comparison of individual differences in e-mail communication, University of Edinburgh. Available at http://homepages.inf.ed.ac.uk/jon/papers/lwc9.pdf. Accessed 4/2/2015.

9   What's in a Name?

1. Eagleman, *Incognito*, p. 62.
2. According to Belgian psychologist Joseph Nuttin.
3. A.J. Splatt and D. Weedon (1977), The Urethral Syndrome: Experience with the Richardson Urethroplasty, *British Journal of Urology*, Vol. 49, No. 2, pp. 173–6; doi:10.1111/j.1464-410X.1977.tb04095.x. PMID 870138.

II   Winning the Emotional Mind

1. D. Westen (2007), *The Political Brain: The Role of Emotion in Deciding the Fate of the Nation*, New York: PublicAffairs.
2. Jill Dan (2012), *Emotional intelligence*, Croydon: Hodder Education, p. 7.

10   Stories and Emotion

1. http://www.physorg.com/print152210728.html. Accessed 20/4/2015.
2. Chip and Dan Heath (2008), *Made to Stick: Why some Ideas Take Hold and Others Come Unstuck*, London: Arrow.
3. Antonio Damasio (2010), *Self Comes to Mind: Constructing the Conscious Brain*, New York: Pantheon, p. 293.
4. This is a running theme in V.S. Ramachandran (2011), *The Tell-Tale Brain: Unlocking the Mystery of Human Nature*, St Ives: William Heinemann.

11   Personal Stories

1. Barack Obama, Back to School speech, 2010.
2. Donald Hebb (1949), *The Organization of Behaviour: A Neuropsychological Theory*, New York: Wiley.
3. James W. Pennebaker (1990), *Opening Up: The Healing Power of Expressing Emotions*, New York: Guilford Press.
4. Dan P. McAdams says that childhood shapes the story of our lives. See: Adams (2008), *The Person: An Introduction to the Science of Personality Pyschology*, New York: Wiley.

12   Creating Cultures

1. The YouTube Gurus – how a couple of regular guys built a company that changed the way we see ourselves, by John Cloud, 25 December 2006. Available at http://content.time.com/time/magazine/article/0,9171,1570795-5,00.html. Accessed 5/2/2015.

14   The Value of Values

1. John Mackey (CEO of Whole Foods) (2014), *Conscious Capitalism*, Boston: Harvard Business Review Press.

15   Great Words We Love

1. Jeffrey Hausdorff, professor of medicine at Harvard University.

16   Flattery and Love

1. https://archive.ama.org/archive/AboutAMA/Pages/AMA%20Publications/ AMA%20Journals/Journal%20of%20Marketing%20Research/TOCs/ SUM_2010.1/Insincere_Flattery_Actually_Works.aspx. Accessed 5/2/2015.
2. http://peakteams.com/blog/understanding-dopamine-3-areas-leaders-can-make-an-impact-on-the-brain/. Accessed 5/2/2015.
3. Robert Cialdini (2007), *Influence: The Psychology of Persuasion*, New York: Harper Business Review Press.
4. http://businesslife.ba.com/Ideas/Trends/The-art-of-flattery.html. Accessed 20/4/2015.
5. http://unhealthywork.org/classic-studies/the-whitehall-study/. Accessed 5/2/2015.
6. S. Sinek (2014), *Leaders Eat Last: Why Some Teams Pull Together and Others Don't*, St Ives: Portfolio Penguin, p. 30.
7. P. Kramer (1997), *Listening to Prozac: A Psychiatrist Explores Antidepressant Drugs and the Remaking of the Self*, London: Penguin Books.

17   Repetition. Repetition. Repetition

1. L. Hasher, D. Goldstein and T. Toppino (1977), Frequency and the Conference of Referential Validity, *Journal of Verbal Learning and Verbal Behavior*, Vol. 16, pp. 107–12.

18   The Eternal Power of Exaggeration

1. Lascaux's Picasso – What prehistoric art tells us about the evolution of the brain, by Katy Waldman. Available at http://www.slate.com/articles/health_and_ science/human_evolution/2012/10/cave_paintings_and_the_human_brain_ how_neuroscience_helps_explain_abstract.html. Accessed 5/2/2015.
2. IPSOS Mori, Perceptions we get wrong, 9 July 2013. Available at https://www. ipsos-mori.com/researchpublications/researcharchive/3188/Perceptions-are-not-reality-the-top-10-we-get-wrong.aspx. Accessed 5/2/2015.

III   Winning the Logical Mind

1. Ming-Zher Puh, Student Member, IEEE, Nicholas C. Swenson and Rosalind W. Picard, Fellow, IEEE (2010), A Wearable Sensor for Unobtrusive, Long-Term Assessment of Electrodermal Activity, *Transactions on Biomedical Engineering*, Vol. 57, No. 5, May. Available at http://affect.media.mit.edu/pdfs/10.Poh-etal-TBME-EDA-tests.pdf. Accessed 13/2/2015.
2. http://www.guardian.co.uk/uk/2004/feb/03/science.highereducation?INTCMP=SRCH. Accessed 12/5/2015.

19   Threes! Threes! Threes!

1. Juan Pablo Vazquez Sampere (2015), We shouldn't be dazzled by Apple's quarterly report, 4 February. Available at https://hbr.org/2015/02/we-shouldnt-be-dazzled-by-apples-earnings-report. Accessed 5/2/2015.
2. Advice first extolled by Speaker Lowther in 1917.
3. As described by Andrew Adonis (2013), *5 Days in May: The Coalition and Beyond*, London: Biteback Publishing, pp. 58–9.
4. General MacArthur, Silvanus Thayer Acceptance Award speech, delivered 12 May 1962 at West Point. Available at http://www.americanrhetoric.com/speeches/douglasmacarthurthayeraward.html. Accessed 12/2/2015.
5. http://www.guardian.co.uk/lifeandstyle/2012/mar/03/mr-tumble-justin-fletcher-gigglebiz. Accessed 12/2/2015.
6. http://www.guardian.co.uk/politics/2005/oct/04/conservatives2005.conservatives3. Accessed 12/2/2015.
7. Russell Brand's interview with Jeremy Paxman on BBC's *Newsnight* in 2013. Available at https://www.youtube.com/watch?v=3YR4CseY9pk. Accessed 12/2/2015.

20   Balance

1. Dick Morris, who worked for Bill Clinton on his 1996 campaign, described triangulation in an interview on *Frontline* in 2000: 'Take the best from each party's agenda, and come to a solution somewhere above the positions of each party. That became a triangle, which was triangulation.' Available at http://www.pbs.org/wgbh/pages/frontline/shows/clinton/interviews/morris2.html. Accessed 27/1/2015.
2. Hippocrates (2010), *Aphorisms*, London: Nabu Press.
3. Osborne, 2011 Budget.

21 Rhyme or Reason

1. M.S. McGlone and J. Tofighbakhsh, source: Department of Psychology, Lafayette College, Easton, PA 18042-1781, USA.
2. Friedrich Nietzsche (2001), *The Gay Science*, New York: Random House.
3. A.J. DeCasper and M.J. Spence (1986), Prenatal Maternal Speech Influences Newborns' Perception of Speech Sounds, *Infant Behavioural Development*, Vol. 9, pp. 133–50.

22 Power of Perspective

1. This is a joke.

23 Think of a Number

1. http://www.telegraph.co.uk/education/maths-reform/9115665/Numeracy-Campaign-17m-adults-struggle-with-primary-school-maths.html. Accessed 13/2/2015.
2. T.D. Wilson (2002), *Strangers to Ourselves: Discovering the Adaptive Instinctive*, Cambridge, MA: Belknap Press of Harvard University Press, p. 24.
3. Stanislas Dehaene (2011), *The Number Sense: How the Mind Creates Mathematics*, New York: Oxford University Press.

Epilogue

1. T.S. Eliot (2001 [1943]), *Four Quartets*, London: Faber and Faber.
2. http://www.dailymail.co.uk/sciencetech/article-2449632/How-check-phone-The-average-person-does-110-times-DAY-6-seconds-evening.html. Accessed 20/4/2015.

Index